Corner House Publishers

SOCIAL SCIENCE REPRINTS

General Editor MAURICE FILLER

G. da Fabriano. St. Nicholas with Conventional Emblems along with Mary Magdalene, St. John, and St. George.

St. Nicholas

His Legend and His Rôle in the Christmas Celebration and Other Popular Customs

By

George H. McKnight

Illustrated

CORNER HOUSE PUBLISHERS

WILLIAMSTOWN, MASSACHUSETTS 01267

1974

FIRST PUBLISHED 1917

REPRINTED 1974

BY

CORNER HOUSE PUBLISHERS

Printed in the United States of America

PREFACE

A FEW years ago, while trying to trace the history of certain Christmas customs, I was unavoidably brought into contact with St. Nicholas. A closer acquaintance with that amiable personality was the result, and acquaintance gradually deepened into veneration and affection. In the same year in which began my closer acquaintance with St. Nicholas, I was so fortunate as to be brought face to face with some of the quaint pictures in which Italian painters, with so much charm, have represented the various episodes in the life of the saint. I was led to believe that others would enjoy the pictures, not all of them readily accessible, and that a wider knowledge of St. Nicholas would greatly enlarge the circle of his friends. The present book was the result.

My aim has been, not to offer an exhaustive study of all the difficult questions that are connected with the name of St. Nicholas, but to bring together, from somewhat scattered sources, the elements in his life story. The kindly acts recorded of him have lived in popular memory and have flowered into some of the most generally cherished of popular customs.   In St. Nicholas the reader will come in contact with a personality of unique amiability, whose influence has permeated popular customs for many centuries and has contributed much of sweetness to human life.

My original contribution to the subject has been slight.   In the notes I have attempted to indicate my indebtedness to other writers, although the amount of this debt I have not been able adequately to show.   To the artists who have represented with feeling and with charm the scenes in the life of St. Nicholas, this book is most indebted, and for them I wish to bespeak a major part of the reader's attention.

G. H. McK.

COLUMBUS, O.,
  July 16, 1917.

CONTENTS

ILLUSTRATIONS

vii

Illustrations

ST. NICHOLAS

CHAPTER I

ST. NICHOLAS, SANTA CLAUS, AND KRIS KRINGLE

THE good St. Nicholas, the bishop-saint, is strangely little known in America. He has lent his name to a church here and there and to a popular magazine for children, his protégés. But how many people are familiar with the story of his life? How many even know the date of his own special festival? There are countries in which his memory is not thus neglected, in which the festival of St. Nicholas is one of the important events of the year. An English newspaper of the first year of the war has this to report concerning the Belgian custom:

The feast of St. Nicholas, December 6th, was celebrated at the Belgian refugee camp at Earle's Court, England, with presents for the children, stockings hung up, a Christmas tree, and all the rest of the children's festivities which we associate with Christmas eve and Christmas morning. This was not a mere anticipation of Christmas. St. Nicholas' day, and not Christmas, is the children's festival in Holland, Belgium, and parts of Germany, and we have borrowed the hanging up of stockings from them and turned it into a Christmas custom.[1]

Letters from Belgian children, exiled in France for more that two years, offer further evidence of the intimate and friendly relationship existing between St. Nicholas and his Belgian children. Here is a touching passage from a letter written by a little eight-year-old Belgian girl from Varengeville-sur-Mer, in France, to an American "godmother"; the adult English used in translation fails to reproduce the naïve charm of the original.

We have just had a grand visit from St. Nicholas. He came in person to bring us some nice things as he used to do when we were home. We were playing when, all at once, we heard singing at one side and saw a bishop, ringing a bell. What joy, it is St. Nicholas! We kneeled down to receive his blessing, and then sang a song and went into the house. St. Nicholas talked to us and, best of all, he gave us some presents. He gave us an orange, a barley sweet, a cake, and some games. My, how happy we were!

GERMAINE BARBEZ.

Le 16 dec., 1916.

Another little girl, a little older, writes from the same place of 'how the "grand Saint Nicholas" has gone out of his way to come to see the Belgian children on December sixth, and how he delivered admonitions to various boys and girls but did not fail to distribute among them dainties much appreciated by all, big and little.'

The importance of St. Nicholas in Belgian life is evident. His festival day too, the celebration of which is so deeply rooted as not to lose its life in an atmosphere of exile and painful memory, has continued to hold an important place in the year's life not only of Belgium but, as remains to be seen, of Holland. At one time the celebration of St. Nicholas' day seems to have been general in most of western Europe. There is plentiful record of the earlier popularity of this celebration in all the southern and western parts of the countries occupied by the peoples speaking the Teutonic languages. It can be traced from Holland and Belgium, through eastern France, the Rhine provinces, Luxembourg, Alsace and Lorraine, through Switzerland, both French and German, as far east as the Tyrol and Salzburg, including on the way Baden, Württemberg, and Bavaria, in Germany.[2] In northern Germany, Protestantism, with its aversion to saint worship, was hostile to the St. Nicholas celebration. Also the growing concentration on Christmas day of the different winter popular celebrations, and especially the rapid rise in importance, during the last two centuries, of the Christmas tree, have caused the St. Nicholas customs, in many places, to be absorbed into the Christmas celebration, in other places, to go quite out of use. But popular customs seem to be to some extent affected by political boundaries, and in two of the smaller countries of western Europe, Belgium and Holland, the St. Nicholas customs still retain much of their earlier vigor.

In Belgium, St. Nicholas has long been among the most venerated of saints, hardly second to St. Martin. In the whole country there are one hundred and six churches in his honor.[3] Besides he is the patron saint of many trades and crafts, for example, of the boatmen in cities on the Meuse, of sawyers, dyers, turners, and haberdashers at Bruges, of seedmen, packers, and coopers at Liège, of haberdashers and mercers at Malines. But above all he is the protector and the corrector of children.

The children's festival at Christmas time does not exist in Belgium. The *grand réveillon*, the great Christmas feast of southern France, which leads children to call Christmas the "day when one eats so much," the English Christmas, with its life and gayety and open hospitality, have nothing corresponding at Christmas time in Belgium,[4] where the celebration of Christmas is confined almost entirely to services in the church. In place of the Christmas gayeties of other countries, Belgium has its St. Nicholas festival. St. Nicholas' day throughout the whole country is a day of joy, especially for the young. Even the German Christmas tree, which has been gradually finding its way into Belgium, is introduced not on Christmas day, but on December 6th, the day devoted to the honor of the popular saint.

A writer of about fifty years back thus describes the joyous celebration of St. Nicholas' day by Belgian children of that time. "Weeks beforehand, children full of impatience, before going to sleep ask: 'How many times must I go to sleep before he comes?' They sing to him as soon as it is dark, and they see him in their dreams, giving them gifts or punishment, according as they have been good or naughty. Occasionally they are made happy by a little gift that comes down the chimney into a pinafore hung up to receive it, or is found accidentally in the corner of the room. A joyful 'Thank you, Saint Nicholas' greets each such gift. Each evening every corner of the room is searched, and the children sing with fervor their petition, one Flemish version of which begins:

'Sint Niklaes, Gods heilge man,
Doe uwen besten tabbaerd aen,
En rydt er mee naer spanje
Om appelen van Oranje
Om peeren van den boom.' "

In one of the versions of this children's song the supplication is addressed to "Sinte Niklaes van Tolentyn," a saint quite distinct from Saint Nicholas of Bari, the recognized patron of children, but the heavenly postal arrangements seem to be effectively organized, for, so far as known, the wrong address used, in no way prevents the desired response from their special protector and friend.

On the eve of his festival day, St. Nicholas makes his tour, visiting palace and cottage. Frequently in the early evening he makes a preliminary visit in bishop's robes, with pastoral staff and miter, at each house making inquiries concerning the conduct of the children, giving appropriate praise or warning, and promising on the following morning to give more substantial reward.

When he is gone, the children place receptacles for the gifts which St. Nicholas is expected to let fall down the chimney. The receptacle varies in different places. Sometimes shoes are neatly polished for the purpose,[5] at other times plates or baskets or stockings or specially made shoes of porcelain are set on the bed, in the open chimney, before the door of a room, or merely in the corner of a room. St. Nicholas' steed, variously conceived of as gray horse or white ass, is not forgotten. For him the children put water and hay or carrot or potato peeling or piece of bread, in the shoe or basket or stocking. In the morning, from the tipped-over chairs and general disarray in the room, it is evident that St. Nicholas has been present. Replacing the oats or hay or carrot are found sweets and playthings for children that have been good, obedient, and studious during the year.[6] In the case of bad children, rods are left, and the fodder is untouched.

A recent writer has given a highly interesting account[7] of the similar celebration at the present day in Holland, where St. Nicholas' day has the same importance as in Belgium.

St. Nicholas' eve is a time of great importance to children because at that time they receive a visit from the saint, and his arrival is looked forward to with trembling. A large white sheet is placed on the floor in the middle of the room, and the children stand about anxiously watching the slow movement of the hands of the clock. In the meantime some of the elder members of the family dress up so as to represent St. Nicholas and his black servant. At five minutes before the expected time, for St. Nicholas generally announces at what time he may be expected, they sing songs asking him to give liberally as is his wont, and praising his greatness and goodness in eloquent terms. The first intimation of his arrival is a shower of sweets on the sheet spread on the floor. Then, amid the ensuing scramble, St. Nicholas appears in full bishop's vestments, laden with presents, while in the rear comes his black servant with an open sack in one hand, for naughty boys and girls, and in the other a rod which he shakes vigorously from time to time. St. Nicholas usually knows the shortcomings of individual children, and on his departure gives each an appropriate lecture, promising to return later. Sometimes he makes the children repeat a verse to him or asks about their lessons.

The mysterious events of the ensuing night closely parallel those recorded for Belgium. St. Nicholas' robe, his "beste tabbaerd," enables him to pass from place to place instantaneously. But in his nightly journey over the roofs of houses, he uses a horse which the children of Holland, like those of Belgium, remember by leaving a wisp of hay for his use.[8] If, for some reason, on account of lack of time or of money, the parents have neglected to buy gifts, the children say, "St. Nicholas' horse has glass legs; he has slipped down and broken his foot."[9]

But the joys of St. Nicholas' eve in Holland are not confined to children. It is a time, like the Christmas season in England, for family reunions and the renewal of old memories, also for the giving of presents. But the manner of the Dutch gift-giving has its distinctive features, for:

St. Nicholas' presents must be hidden and disguised as much as possible and be accompanied by rhymes explaining what the gift is, and for whom St. Nicholas intended it. Sometimes a parcel addressed to one person will finally turn out to be for quite a different member of the family from the one who first received it. For the address on each wrapper in various stages of wrapping, makes it necessary for the parcel to change hands as many times as there are papers to undo. Tiniest things are sent in immense packing cases. Sometimes the gifts are baked in a loaf of bread or hidden in a turf. The longer it takes to find the present, the greater the surprise.

Great delight is taken in concealing the identity of the giver as long as possible. Even if the gift comes from a member of the same household, before the parcel is brought in, the doorbell is rung by a servant in order to create the impression that the par-

cel has come from an outsider.   For the same purpose
a parcel for a friend's house is often entrusted to a
passer-by.

On the evening of the celebration, after St. Nicholas
has said his adieux, promising to come again, the
children are packed away to bed, and the older people
have their special amusement.   They sit about a table
in the middle of the room and partake of tea and
"speculaas," a spice cake bearing a great picture of
St. Nicholas, until their own surprises begin to arrive.
When this part of the program is over, about ten
o'clock, the room is cleared; the dust sheet laid down
for the children's scramble, is removed, the papers,
boxes, baskets, and the like, used in packing the
presents, are cleared away.   The table is spread with
a white tablecloth, and when all have taken seats,
a dish of boiled chestnuts, steaming hot, is brought
in and eaten with butter and salt.[10]

Belgium and Holland have their special forms
of cakes and sweetmeats for the St. Nicholas
season.   In Holland these are the flat hard cakes
called "Klaasjes"[11] once made exclusively in the
form of a bishop in honor of the bishop St. Nicholas, but now made in forms of every conceivable
kind of beast, bird, or fish.   In certain places on
the Rhine the figure of the saint himself, the "Klas-
mann," is baked in dough with currant eyes,
or an especially palatable little horse is formed of
honey cake dough and the "Klas" is inlaid on the

horse. Then there is the "Letterbanket" made in the form of letters so that one may order his name in cake, and the "Marsepein," now made in a great variety of forms, but formerly made only in heart-shaped sweets ornamented with little turtle doves made of pink sugar or with a flaming heart on a little altar. The "Marsepein" was formerly used as a device in wooing. The young man sent "Marsepein"[12] with a "Vryer" of cake to the young lady of his heart, and if she accepted, he knew his cause was won.

There are also various accounts of the way the cakes are made. In Vorarlberg if, on the morning of St. Nicholas' day, mist is seen to rise, one tells the children that St. Nicholas is baking his cakes, "Zelten" or "Klösse." All the different figures found on the "Zelten" have been made by St. Nicholas' ass stepping on them with his shoes. Another explanation of the origin of the cakes has more direct relation with the life story of the saint. The story is told that the three maidens rescued from shame by St. Nicholas — whose story remains to be told in a later chapter—at their marriage, out of gratitude, baked triple kneaded rolls and distributed them among poor children.[13]

Outside the homes, the time about St. Nicholas'

day in Belgium and Holland is one of unusual
life and gayety.

The old-time St. Nicholas fairs are no longer held
in the streets, at any rate, not in the large towns of
Holland, but exchange of presents is as universal as
ever, and the shops are as festive in appearance as
American shops at Christmas time.[14]   New attrac-
tions for children are offered each year.   Life-sized
figures of St. Nicholas are frequent in front of shop
windows, and some establishments have a man dressed
like the good saint, who goes about the streets mounted
on a white steed, while behind him follows a cart
laden with presents to be delivered.   Crowds of
children, singing, shouting, and clapping their hands,
follow.[15]

An older authority records concerning Belgium
that often in country districts this or that peasant
makes up as a long-bearded man or bishop and
rides through the dark streets on a gray horse,
or an ass, or a wooden horse, with a great basket
at his side and a bundle of whips in his hand.[16]

In no countries besides Belgium and Holland
is the celebration of St. Nicholas' day so widely
prevalent to-day.   But, as already remarked, in
earlier times the celebration of St. Nicholas' day
was popular in many parts of Teutonic Europe,
particularly in Austria, Switzerland, and southern
Germany.   In various parts of these countries

St. Nicholas in East Frisia.

Reproduced from Reinsberg-Düringsfeld, *Das festliche Jahr.*

the old St. Nicholas customs still maintain a vigorous existence. In Württemberg and Baden, children on St. Nicholas' day receive gifts from their godparents. In Switzerland the gifts are brought by "Samiklaus," in the Tyrol by the "Holy Man," in lower Austria by "Niglo," in Bohemia by "Nikolo."[17] At Ehingen on the Danube, it is the custom to keep tally on a stick of the number of prayers the children have said. The child that can show many tallies is favored by Santiklos. Before going to bed children place bowls under the bed and say the prayer:

> "St. Nikolaus, leg mir ein,
> Was dein guter Will mag sein,
> Aepfel, Birnen, Nuss und Kern
> Essen die kleinen Kinder gern.
>
> (St. Nicholas put in for me
> What thy good will may be,
> Apple, pear, and good sweetmeat,
> Little children love to eat.)"

In the morning the bowls are found filled with the good things desired.

In various places in Germany, Switzerland, and Austria, the saint, represented by some older member of the family, appears, or used to appear, in person, in bishop's guise with staff and miter, and makes inquiry concerning the behavior of the children, and hears the children say their prayers. Before his coming the children have placed shoes in the garden behind a bush, and when after his departure they go out, they find the shoes filled with apples, nuts, and the like, if their conduct has been good. But in the case of ill-behaved children, the shoes are likely to be occupied by a whip.

In Italy a similar custom was formerly observed among people of higher social station. In the courts of princes, on St. Nicholas' day, it was a custom to hide presents "in the shoes and slippers of persons whom it was desired to honor, in such manner as to surprise them when they came to dress. The custom was called Zopata from a Spanish word signifying a shoe."[18]

The function of St. Nicholas, it will have been observed, is a double one, to bring pleasing rewards to good children, but also to bring fear to children whose conduct has been bad. A Swiss dialect dictionary published in 1806, defines "Samiklaus" as a "gift such as parents make to their children through a disguised person named Samiklaus (corrupted from St. Nicholas) in order to give them pleasure and encourage them to duty and obedience or to frighten them through the strangely frightful make-up of the bogey man who accompanies the Samiklaus."[19]   As a means of exciting fear in the ill-behaved children, the friendly bishop was often accompanied on his rounds by a children's bugaboo, a frightful figure with horns, black face, fiery eyes, and long red tongue, variously called Klaubauf, Krampus, Rumpanz, and the like.[20]

Further evidence of the earlier wider prevalence of St. Nicholas customs is afforded by the objections[21] of seventeenth-century Protestant preachers, quoted in a later chapter, who opposed the attribution to St. Nicholas of gifts which, they asserted, came from the Christ Child alone. In objections such as these, is to be found one of the causes of the decay of distinctively St. Nicholas customs.   Or perhaps we may better say, here is an explanation why customs that persisted, lost their association with the name of St. Nicholas.   There is apparent Protestant objection to saint worship.   There is also in evidence the rivalry of the celebration in honor of the birth of Christ which had received the name Christmas. The Christmas celebration was in its origin a church affair.   Up to the fourteenth century the church had tried in vain to convert it into a popular festival.   It employed all kinds of methods to attract the traditional customs and beliefs of the beginning of winter to the church festival. But only after the beliefs and practices earlier attached to Martinmas, to St. Andrew's day, and to St. Nicholas' day were brought into association with the birth of Christ, did the Christmas festival, after the end of the fourteenth century, become a genuinely popular occasion.

From this time on the customs distinctive of St. Nicholas' day became more and more absorbed into the Christmas festival.[22] At times St. Nicholas retains his association with the old customs, but the time is shifted from St. Nicholas' day to Christmas time. In Catholic Nuremberg, for instance, at the end of the seventeenth century, the St. Nicholas gift-giving and the Christmas gift-giving customs were united, and the St. Nicholas customs made dependent on the Christmas customs. Children believed that St. Nicholas was the attendant of the Christ Child and was made to carry the wares basket at the Christmas market, and that St. Nicholas received sweetmeats as extras from the dealers. As Christmas time approached, these were put under the pillows of the children, who believed them to be the gifts of St. Nicholas.[23]

In all north Germany, too, on Christmas eve, there goes about a bearded man covered with a great hide or with straw, who questions children and rewards their good conduct. His name varies with the locality. In many places he is called "Knecht Ruprecht," a name probably going back to a pre-Christian time before St. Nicholas became associated with the children's festival. In other places the man is called "De Hele Christ," Holy Christ, who later becomes the central figure of all Christmas activities. In many of his names, however, such as "Rû Clås," "Joseph Clås," "Clåwes,"[24] "Clås Bûr," and "Bullerclås," one will recognize the juvenile derivative from the name Nicholas. This figure often rides on a white horse. Not infrequently his relation to the Christmas festival proper needs to be made clear by the presence of the Holy Christ as a companion, represented by a maiden in white garb who hears the children say their prayers.

Saint Nicholas in the double rôle of children's benefactor and children's bugaboo found his way to America. Among the Pennsylvania Germans, or "Pennsylvania Dutch," as they are more familiarly called, at least in the country districts, he continues to play his old part. "You'd better look out or Pelznickel will catch you," is the threat held out over naughty children about Christmas time. The nickel in Pelznickel serves to show the relationship of this personage to St. Nicholas. Pelznickel is a Santa Claus with some variations. "On Christmas eve someone in the neighborhood impersonates Pelznickel by dressing up as an old man with a long white beard. Arming himself with a switch and carrying a bag of toys over his shoulder, he goes from house to house, where the children are expecting him.

"He asks the parents how the little ones have behaved themselves during the year. To each of those who have been good, he gives a present from his bag. But woe betide the naughty ones! These are not only supposed to get no presents, but Pelznickel catches them by the collar and playfully taps them with his switch."[25]

Eventually, in many places, St. Nicholas became quite excluded from the customs with which he was long associated. In Schleswig-Holstein, for instance, at the beginning of the nineteenth century, the old customs were preserved but entirely separated from their earlier associations with St. Nicholas and St. Nicholas' eve, and now connected with the story of the Christ Child and His festival, Christmas. The custom was for each child to borrow a plate or bowl from the kitchen and place this in an appointed room or in a window. On Christmas eve, when the tinkle

Christkindchen (Kris Kringle) and Hans Trapp in Alsace.
Reproduced from Reinsberg-Düringsfeld, *Das festliche Jahr.*

of the bell summoned the children from the dark anteroom into the room with the festal decorations, then each child found what the Christ Child ("Kindjes") had brought him. On the plates lay cakes, fruits, and playthings. Perhaps a rod was laid beside the other gifts, but it counted as the most severe punishment when the plate remained empty.

Here and there also in the country, as late as 1865, there survived the similar custom, for the children, before going to bed, to place the plate before the window, for in the night the Christ Child took out a pane of glass and laid his gifts on the plate so that on Christmas morning it was evident that the "Kindjes" had been present. Here we see St. Nicholas quite deprived of his old prerogatives and his place taken by the "Christ Kindjes," or as he was called in some places "Christ kindel," from whose name, by a process of popular etymology, presumably was derived the name Kris Kringle.

In various parts of the United States where Dutch and German customs prevail, Kris Kringle appears in the combined rôle of the Christ Child and Santa Claus, and the vigil of his festival is called "Christ Kinkle eve." In certain parts of Germany children sing, on Christmas eve:

"Christkindchen komm;
Mach mich fromm;
Dass ich zu dir im Himmel komm."[26]

In the principality of Waldeck[27] down as late as 1830 there survived a popular Christmas mummers' play custom originating in the sixteenth century and bringing in not only Christ and St. Nicholas but other personages grotesque in appearance, some of them survivals from folk celebrations antedating St. Nicholas customs. In the play appear Christ, Mary, an Angel, Peter, and Niklawes, all clad in white, and Hansruhbart, Brose, who bears the sack, and the shepherd Pamphilius with the noble steed, Zink. Hansruhbart and Brose are clad in pea straw and wear frightful masks. Pamphilius has suspended from a strap about his neck a box full of dirt with which he threatens to smear the children. Each person in turn is summoned to speak. As the chief offence in the case of children is reckoned the preference of small beer to coffee. Peter distributes the gifts, which the children receive only after they have been forgiven. He has a basket with apples and nuts, which he throws on a table for the children. As the children reach out for his gifts, he strikes them on the fingers with his rod.

Mumming pieces like this were popular all over Germany, the personages varying with the locality. Sometimes the Holy Christ went about alone, and before him the children presented themselves. But the most striking of all the personages in these plays was the one at Waldeck called Hansruhbart, elsewhere Ruprecht and Knecht Ruprecht, at his earliest recorded appearance called Acesto, probably a traditional figure that originated in customs that antedate Christianity.

In all this discussion of various customs associated with the name of St. Nicholas there will have been seen little to connect with the life story of a saintly person. The deeds of the children's friend, St. Nicholas, to be sure exhibit beneficence, but the beneficence of a capricious, fairy-like benefactor rather than of a holy saint. In fact it is evident that the customs in question, in their origin, had little, if anything to do with St. Nicholas, and as they exist to-day show only in certain external features any relation with the life story of the kindly Eastern saint. This impression of the earlier independence of the popular customs in question from the story of St. Nicholas, is confirmed by the fact that many of them are associated with other names. St. Martin, as

well as St. Nicholas, figures as a giver of gifts to
children, especially in the Netherlands. At Antwerp and certain other cities, according to a report
from a generation ago, on St. Martin's day, as in
the St. Nicholas' day celebration already described,
a man with bishop's vestments and crosier appeared in the nurseries and made inquiries about
the behavior of the children. According to the
nature of this report he threw on the floor from
his basket, either rods, or apples, nuts, and cakes.
In Ypres children are reported to hang stockings
filled with hay in the open chimneypiece on the
eve of Martinmas. The next morning the stockings are found filled with gifts from St. Martin
who in the night has ridden over the chimney and
has been grateful for the attention paid to his gray
(or white) steed.[28] There is also an old custom
in Flemish Belgium in which on the eve of Martinmas the children are placed in the corner of a
room with their backs to the door and told not
to look. The parents then throw in at the door
apples, nuts, peppercakes, and other sweetmeats
of various kinds, pretending that St. Martin has
done it. If one of the children turns around,
St. Martin goes away without leaving anything.

The bugaboo feature of St. Nicholas' day also
was not lacking in the Martinmas celebration.

In several places in southern Germany, on St. Martin's day, "Pelzmärte," with blackened face and cowbells, went about giving beatings or throwing apples into rooms, whichever the children's behavior called for.

Some of the Martinmas customs had less resemblance to St. Nicholas customs. The convivial customs of Martinmas have given St. Martin a reputation for drunkenness entirely undeserved by that zealous defender of Christianity, St. Martin of Tours. But the ones singled out for mention evidently belong jointly to St. Martin and St. Nicholas, although in their origin probably as little connected with the one as with the other.

The celebration of St. Andrew's day, also, has features similar to that of St. Nicholas' day. On St. Andrew's eve (November thirtieth), in the neighborhood of Reichenberg, children are said to hang up their stockings at the windows and in the evening find them filled with apples and nuts.[29]

The explanation of the origin of these customs is to be found in practices long antedating the time of St. Martin or St. Nicholas or even of St. Andrew. They seem to be practices rooted in pre-Christian agricultural rites which have been superseded, or better expressed, have survived with new meanings read into them. With the introduction of Christianity, following the usual course of things, the older modes of celebration were changed not so much in form as in name. To St. Martin were devoted customs which coincided in time with the celebration in honor of St. Martin, customs originally associated with the first drinking of the new wine or with the autumn slaughter, a connection not entirely lost in our own times, as indicated by the "Martlemas beef" in Great Britain, the "St. Martin's geese" and "St. Martin's swine" in Germany. With the shifting of the agricultural practices to a later date, the customs came to be associated with the celebration of saints' days later in the calendar. With St. Nicholas, on December sixth, became associated customs and practices earlier associated with St. Martin, on November eleventh, or with St. Andrew on November thirtieth, but in their true nature as little appropriate to one as to the other.

There have been attempts to show points of connection between the Christian worship of St. Nicholas and the earlier worship of the Teutonic divinities. It has been attempted to connect the children's bugaboo variously called Hansruhbart, Ruprecht, and Knecht Ruprecht, with Odin,

largely through a connection between the name
Ruprecht and one of the variety of names given
Odin.[30] There has been pointed out also the
parallelism between the "beste tabbaerd" of St.
Nicholas sung about by children, and the magic
robe which enabled Odin to pass from place to
place; between the gray horse of St. Nicholas on
which he rode over the roofs of houses, and Odin's
horse, Sleipnir, on which he took an autumn ride
through the world; between the sheaf of grain in
pagan days left in the field for Odin's horse and
the wisp of hay left by children in their shoes for
their friend St. Nicholas. But too much stress
must not be laid on these parallelisms. The customs
associated with St. Nicholas in their origin doubtless antedate Christianity but also antedate the
worship of Odin. Possibly the pre-Christian
practices were influenced by their temporary
association with the Teutonic gods as they after-
wards were by the association with the Christian
saints. But in both cases this influence was only
superficial.

A rapid resumé may clear up some of the ob-
scure places in the preceding mass of details. In
the practices associated in our time with the name
of Santa Claus we have survivals of pagan sacred
custom once regarded as important in the further-

ance of human welfare. Perhaps influenced superficially by conceptions of the Germanic gods, eventually they came to be connected with the honor of Christian saints. They afford a remarkable illustration of the longevity of folk customs. With meaning lost or changed, the older forms persist. Influenced, as remains to be shown, superficially, by the life story of the saint with whose worship they became associated, also to some extent with the Roman festivities of the same season, above all converted to the use of providing pleasure, as well as just reward, for children, they have survived to our day. But owing in part to the effort of the Church in earlier times to convert the church ceremony in honor of the birth of Christ into a truly popular festival, in part to the later opposition to saint worship on the part of Protestantism, the customs once associated with the worship of St. Nicholas are now associated with the birth of Christ.

Santa Claus, the name derived from St. Nicholas through the familiar use of children in Teutonic countries, crossed to America. The exact route followed by him is somewhat open to question. On the way he traded his gray horse or ass for a reindeer and made changes in his appearance. It is usually said, however, that he was brought to

America by the Dutch.   In America he has made himself very much at home, and according to the explanation most generally accepted, from America he recrossed the Atlantic to England, whence he has journeyed to the most distant parts of the British Empire, to India and to Australia, where he is as familiarly known as in America.   In England, however, while the custom of giving gifts to children has been made a part of the Christmas celebration, the gratitude of the children in some places goes to Santa Claus, but in other places goes to another creation of the popular fancy, a personage called Father Christmas.   In parts of the German-speaking countries also, as has been shown, the honors of Christmas day are concentrated in the person of the Christ Child, and the benefactor of children is the Christ Child himself, the "Kindjes" or "Christ kindel," more familiarly known in America as Kris Kringle. In France the place of the Christ Child as the purveyor of gifts had been in part filled by "le petit Noël," in a manner like that in which in England Father Christmas in part shares the rôle of Santa Claus.

CHAPTER II

BIOGRAPHY AND LEGEND

IT is quite apparent that the journeys of Santa Claus by night over the housetops, and his various chimney escapades, are beneath the dignity of the reverend Bishop of Myra, formally canonized by the medieval church as St. Nicholas. In appearance, too, Santa Claus is more like an elf, or one of the other beings of Teutonic mythology, than like the Christian bishop whom early artists were fond of representing in full episcopal vestments, with miter, pallium, and pastoral staff. In his manners, too, he is more like a friendly fairy than a patron saint. In reality, as has been seen, in his origin there is more of the pagan than of the Christian. At the same time Christian legend has had its influence. The name Santa Claus is a popular, or juvenile, derivative from St. Nicholas, and the mysterious visit by night which wins for Santa Claus the hearts of children, is closely associated with a famous incident in the life story of the Christian saint.

28

What then do we know about St. Nicholas? "Of all patron saints," says Mrs. Jameson, "he is perhaps the most universally popular and interesting. No saint in the calendar has so many churches, chapels, and altars dedicated to him. In England, I suppose, there is hardly a town without one church at least bearing his name." Both in Eastern Church and Western Church he is the object of extreme veneration, to a degree unequalled in the case of any other saint.[1] It is established that veneration of St. Nicholas goes back to the early centuries in the history of the Christian faith. The Emperor Justinian built a church in his honor at Constantinople about the year 430, and he was titular saint of four churches at Constantinople.[2]

Yet with all this high esteem and veneration through so many centuries, little is known concerning the facts of his life. Historical criticism has demolished much of the story built up around his lovable personality. One by one the cherished tales of his beneficence have been questioned, because lacking the required corroboration of historical evidence. There has even been raised doubt whether he ever existed. In any case certain knowledge is extremely dim. The authorized story of his life set as the *lectio* or "reading" for the second nocturn of St. Nicholas' day (Dec. 6th) in the Roman Breviary, makes but a slight narrative. In brief paraphrase it runs as follows:

An only child, in infancy he manifested singular piety. His youth was characterized by deeds of charity, among them one that saved three maidens from a life of shame. In youth, on a sea voyage, he saved the ship in a fearful storm. In youth also he was elected Bishop of Myra, a miraculous sign indicating him to be the divine choice. In later life he succored the oppressed, in particular saving three tribunes unjustly condemned to death. At the Council of Nice he is said to have condemned the Arian heresy, and at his death is said to have received miraculous sign of divine approval. His remains are preserved with the greatest veneration at Bari in Italy.

This sober biography, so lacking in concrete detail, is the life of the beloved saint as sanctioned by the Roman Church of to-day. As already remarked, most even of its meager details have been questioned by higher criticism. In earlier times, however, when the test of reality was not as rigorously applied as is the wont to-day, there flourished a luxuriant growth of stories about St. Nicholas as about other saints, the objects of popular veneration and gratitude.

Much is to be said in favor of the earlier, more imaginative, lives of the saints, *legends* as they were technically called. It has been remarked, with much truth, that all of us lead double lives, a life of our fancy, in a world of things as they should be, or as we should like them to be, and a life in a world of things as they really are. And this is as it should be. We can lift the level of real existence by thinking of things as we should like them to be. It is well not to walk with one's eyes always fixed on the ground. The uplift to be derived from the contemplation of things as they should be as distinguished from things as they are, is well exemplified in the case of the legendary stories about St. Nicholas. The fact that these largely imaginative stories existed in the belief of people served to influence human action, leading to imitation which eventually crystallized into some of the noblest of popular customs. In some of the beautiful popular customs connected with the name of St. Nicholas we have the projection into reality of fanciful stories once held worthy of implicit faith.

Much deserves to be said also in favor of the creators of legendary story. One is sometimes disposed to look on such story uncharitably and to regard it as the product of willful intent to deceive. Such is by no means the real explanation of the origin of legendary tales. Such tales are usually the product of intense emotional life, when the imagination becomes heated by prolonged contemplation of any subject. Thus we must explain the revelations to St. Francis and the vivid scenes from the life of Christ attributed to St. Bonaventura. A similar condition serves to explain the popular capacity for belief in tales of the supernatural. We sometimes think of such legendary story as the exclusive product of an earlier, uncritical age. That we are mistaken in this opinion and that the conditions for the production of legendary story continue to exist in our own time, is illustrated in a striking manner by certain highly interesting stories that owe, if not their origin, at least their circulation, to the intensity of feeling aroused by the war in Europe. There has found wide circulation a story concerning certain supernatural occurrences on the battlefield of Mons. "The story goes that at the crisis of the fighting, when the French and English were growing disheartened by their ineffectual efforts to overcome the enemy, certain celestial beings, in the midst of whom was St. George, suddenly appeared between the armies and by their timely aid brought victory to the Allies".[3] The origin of this story has been clearly explained. Its author, Arthur Machen, in a recent volume, gives a circumstantial account of its creation. It "was conceived and written by me," he tells us, "in prosaic London, on the last Sunday of August, 1914," immediately after reading of the retreat from Mons, and this story, for which he chose the title, "The Bowmen," was published in *The Evening News* of September 29th the same year. This story then, an admitted fiction, has nevertheless found life in popular belief. It has found not only oral circulation but has been reproduced in print with variants and corroborative testimony. In its circulation it has reached the outermost bounds of the British Empire. How a story which under ordinary conditions would at once be recognized as fiction, now finds ready credence, is revealed in the following extract from a personal letter from far-away Sydney in Cape Breton:

Rev. Mr. —— preached in Falmouth Street Church on Sunday night on the Angels at Mons. I had seen in the papers that the Allies had seen three figures in the sky in the retreat from Mons and that although the Germans pursued them, they never could catch up with them. But I just thought it some Roman Catholic superstition. But Mr. —— thought otherwise. He said reliable people on both sides had undoubtedly seen them, and he thought the age of miracles is not yet past and that if anyone had told him two years ago that he would have been preaching to justify this vision he would have thought him crazy. I really never heard a more wonderful sermon. Rev. Mr. —— has enlisted and goes overseas with the 85th.

The origin of such a miraculous tale and of others of the same kind, such as that of the "Comrade in White," and the credence given in our own time, by critical, skeptical Protestants, enable one to understand the origin of earlier stories of the supernatural and how in less critical times general credence could be attached to stories to the unsympathetic now often seeming preposterous.

The Church, too, in earlier times was not rigorous in the exclusion of extravagant features in the life history of its heroes. On the contrary it permitted the fancy to play freely about the objects of its veneration, was hospitable to the wonderful, the supernatural, element in story. By various means it aimed to keep ever alive the memory of the saints, not excluding the livelier details contributed by popular tradition. Legendary stories in Latin prose formed a part of the private reading of the clergy in their canonical hours, and in vernacular prose or verse were read before popular congregations in church on the days devoted to the honor of the particular saint.

Scenes from the Legend of St. Nicholas in the Stained Glass (thirteenth century) of Bourges Cathedral.

Reproduced from Paul Lacroix, *Science and Art of the Middle Ages.*

Sometimes they found a place in the story reper-
tory of secular minstrels. Artists other than
literary contributed their share toward the per-
petuation of the legendary story. The separate
scenes in the lives of the popular saints were presented in stained glass windows, particularly in
France,[4] in series of pictures on canvas, in
wall paintings adorning the chapels devoted to
particular saints, especially in Italy, or in sculptured series, in low or in high relief, as architectural
ornament or decorating the sides of baptismal fonts
as in the case of the St. Nicholas scenes represented
in the fonts at Winchester cathedral and elsewhere
in England and on the continent.

In even more effective ways the stories were
kept alive when the principal scenes were re-
enacted in dramatic entertainments, by towns
or guilds in honor of their particular patron saints,
or by schoolboys in honor of their patron Saint
Nicholas.

In all these ways the story of St. Nicholas was
kept in memory. Of Eastern origin, St. Nicholas
became the object of general veneration in the
West, especially after the transfer of his remains
to Bari in Italy in the year 1087. The especial
honor paid to him doubtless finds its explanation
in the nature of his life story and the particular

needs of earlier times. In the days when the idea that God is love had not become the central feature of Christianity, when God was regarded rather as a judge, just but therefore severe, suffering humanity felt the need of a more approachable divine personality. This place of intermediary between man and divine justice was taken in part by Our Lady, the Divine Mother, and almost countless are the *Miracles de Notre Dame*, the tales of aid afforded by her to human beings in distress. A similar part was played to some extent by each of the popular saints, but above all by St. Nicholas, who was the principal agent in many stories of this kind.

It is my purpose, then, to take up in detail the story of St. Nicholas as found in these earlier records, which reflect so well the devotion felt for the most thoroughly human of all the saints. Though many elements pass the bounds of modern credulity, they serve to express the loving reverence felt for the saint who, second only to Our Lady herself, was looked to as the beneficent source of aid in times of human distress, and at the same time serve to explain some of the most interesting of popular customs.

CHAPTER III

THE BOY ST. NICHOLAS AND ST. NICHOLAS THE
PATRON SAINT OF SCHOOLBOYS

THE legendary story of St. Nicholas has certain
features that distinguish it from the legendary stories of other saints. The story of St.
Nicholas is not a narrative of a single dramatic
achievement, like that in the life of St. George,
nor of a glorious martyrdom, like that of a St.
Sebastian or a St. Cecilia. Nor is the name of
St. Nicholas associated with the diffusion of the
Christian faith like that of St. Augustine, St.
Boniface, or St. Patrick, nor with the exposition
of Christian doctrine, like that of St. Jerome or
St. Bernard. More like, it is yet different from,
that story of perfect exemplification of the Christian life, the life story of St. Francis. The story
of St. Nicholas consists almost entirely of a series
of beneficent deeds, of aid afforded humanity in
distress, accomplished either by St. Nicholas
during his lifetime or through his intervention

after death. As a benefactor he ranks almost with Divinity in his aid rendered, and even lacks the severity of the justice that attends Divine awards.

The conception of St. Nicholas, then, is almost that of beneficence incarnate. The minor traits of his personality, however, the nature of his parentage, the time details in his life history, the exact manner of his death, are left in comparative obscurity. The very vagueness of the information concerning him serves in great measure to explain the remarkable variety of the rôles he has assumed in the world's history. Only the nebulous ideas that have prevailed concerning him have made it possible that in Scandinavia his name should be connected with that of a hostile water demon, known in English as the "Old Nick," while in certain parts of Siberia he receives divine honor and is worshiped as the "Russian god Nicolo." A similar reason explains how he comes to be regarded as patron saint of classes of people as dissimilar as schoolboys, parish clerks, unwedded maids, seamen, pirates, and thieves, how it is possible to associate him with the whimsical children's friend Santa Claus.

The story of the boyhood of St. Nicholas, reverent in tone and not a little tinged with the

Beato Angelico.   Three Scenes from the Early Life of St. Nicholas.

supernatural, is of the kind that one might well look for in the legendary account of one whose memory is entirely associated with kindness and generosity. St. Nicholas was born, the Golden Legend[1] tells us, 'in the city of Patras in Asia Minor, of rich and holy kin. His father was Epiphanes, and his mother Johane. He was begotten in the first flower of their age, and from that time forthon they lived in continence and led an heavenly life.' From the first the boy Nicholas manifested signs of extreme piety, observing fasting periods even in earliest infancy. The story runs: "Then, the first day that he was washed and bained, he addressed himself right up in the bason, and he would not take the breast nor the pap but once on Wednesday and once on Friday, and in his young age he eschewed the plays and japes of other young children. He used and haunted gladly holy church; and all that he might understand of holy scripture, he executed it in deed and work after his power." Thus he is represented in the narrative of the Golden Legend. Thus too he is represented in the series of scenes painted by Beato Angelico and preserved in the Vatican gallery. In these interesting paintings there is a scene respresenting the infant Nicholas at the time of his birth standing up in the basin, and a second scene where he is represented in a flower-covered ground in front of a church, devoutly standing in front of a group of worshipers listening to the words of a bishop who preaches from above in an outside pulpit. Chaucer's Prioress, speaking of the saintly boy murdered by the Jews, remarks:

> "But ay, when I remembre on this matere,
> Seint Nicholas stant ever in my presence,
> For he so yong to Christ did reverence."

It is not hard to see why he should have been chosen as patron saint of children, unless, indeed, the story of his pious childhood itself originates from the fact that he was the patron saint of children. In the words of the English *Liber Festivalis*, "his parents called him Nycolas, that is a mannes name, but he kepeth the name of a child, for he chose to kepe vertue, meknes, and simplenes, and without malice. . . . And therefore, children don him worship before all other saints."

But it is to be feared that the exemplary boyhood of St. Nicholas would hardly in itself have sufficed to give him so firm a hold on the affections of children. Children of our day, or shall we say of the day that has just passed, in the stories provided them, not infrequently read of boys almost equally exemplary, without being unduly moved to love, reverence, or emulation. A more sure road to the affections of children is through benefits received or at least stories of benefits rendered. Children love and honor St. Nicholas because they conceive of the spirit of St. Nicholas as a guardian angel, not only looking after their safety and well-being, but bringing them substantial rewards, and many of the stories told of him, led children to feel toward him the warmest gratitude and at the same time to look to him as a semi-divine protector in time of trouble.

St. Nicholas was particularly the patron saint of schoolboys, and one of the best known of the stories of protection afforded by him is thus told in the Golden Legend:[2]

A man, for the love of his son, that went to school for to learn, hallowed, every year, the feast of S. Nicholas much solemnly. On a time it happed that the father had to make ready the dinner, and called many clerks [schoolboys] to this dinner. And the devil came to the gate in the habit of a pilgrim for to demand alms; and the father anon commanded his son that he should give alms to the pilgrim. He followed him as he went for to give him alms, and when he came to the quarfox the devil caught the child and strangled him. And when the father heard this he sorrowed much strongly and wept, and bare the body into his chamber, and began to cry for sorrow, and say: Bright sweet son, how is it with thee? S. Nicholas, is this the guerdon that ye have done to me because I have so long served you? And as he said these words, and other semblable, the child opened his eyes, and awoke like as he had been asleep, and arose up before all, and was raised from death to life.

The clerks assembled at the dinner in honor of St. Nicholas, the devil in pilgrim guise seeking alms at the door, and later strangling the boy who has followed him outside, and the boy on the bed being brought to life through influence of his protector saint, all with entire disregard to unity of time, are represented in one of the animated scenes of the painting by Lorenzetti in Florence, in which in quaintly primitive fashion is anticipated the method of the modern motion picture.

Another story with St. Nicholas in his favorite rôle is thus told in the Golden Legend:

There was another rich man that by the merits of S. Nicholas had a son and called him: *Deus dedit*, "God gave." And this rich man did do make a chapel of S. Nicholas in his dwelling place; and did do hallow every year the feast of S. Nicholas. And this manor was set by the land of the Agarians. This

A. Lorenzetti.   The Young Clerk Strangled by the Devil at the Feast
on St. Nicholas' Eve and Brought to Life by the Saint.

child was taken prisoner, and deputed to serve the king. The year following, and the day that the father held devoutly the feast of S. Nicholas, the child held a precious cup tofore the king, and remembered his prise, the sorrow of his friends, and the joy that was made that day in the house of his father, and began to sigh sore high. And the king demanded him what ailed him and the cause of his sighing; and he told him every word wholly. And when the king knew it, he said to him; Whatsomever thy Nicholas do or do not, thou shalt abide here with us. And suddenly there blew a much strong wind, that made all the house to tremble, and the child was ravished with the cup, and was set tofore the gate where his father held the solemnity of S. Nicholas, in such wise that they all demeaned great joy.

A variant version of this story is included in the Golden Legend. It runs as follows:

And some say that this child was of Normandy, and went oversea, and was taken by the sowdan, which made him oft to be beaten before him. And as he was beaten on a S. Nicholas day, and was set in prison, he prayed to S. Nicholas as well for the beating that he suffered, as for the great joy that he was wont to have on that day of S. Nicholas. And when he had long prayed and sighed, he fell asleep, and when he awoke he found himself in the chapel of his father, whereas much joy was made for him.

Wace, the twelfth-century author of a life of St. Nicholas in French verse, supplies the introductory part of this story only briefly alluded to in the Golden Legend version. He tells of the rich merchant of Alexandria named Getro, and his wife, Eufrosine, who have longed in vain for children. Getro hears of St. Nicholas and goes to the city where St. Nicholas lives, to seek his aid. But he finds the saint dead and on his bier. He asks for some of the saint's clothes. These he bears as holy relics to Alexandria and erects a church for them. The next December, on St. Nicholas' day, a son is born and receives the name Deudoné. This son is carried off by robbers and sold to the emperor, whom he serves as cup-bearer. On St. Nicholas' day the boy weeps but is cruelly beaten for it. At the same time his father in Alexandria is praying to St. Nicholas, and on rising from prayer, finds his son, safely restored, standing before him. After that, natu-rally, there is no neglect to worship St. Nicholas on his festival day.

This story seems to be closely connected with the development of St. Nicholas worship in western Europe following the removal of his relics to Bari, Italy. General veneration of the saint, long popular in the East, seems to increase in the West after that event. The particular incident just recorded is followed in Wace by these words:

> Devant ceo ne trovons pas
> qui si servist saint Nicholas,

which may be translated, "Before this we do not find worshipers of Saint Nicholas," and seem to indicate that the composition of Wace was connected in some way with a newly instituted church festival.

The story was one kept particularly in memory since, as remains to be seen, it formed the subject of a schoolboy play enacted by the boys on St. Nicholas' eve. It also forms the subject of two of the scenes in fresco, possibly by Giottino, possibly by Giotto himself, as a young man, in the church of St. Francis at Assisi. The first scene in these frescoes represents a boy prisoner of a Saracen king in the act of raising a cup to his lord seated at table, when St. Nicholas, hovering above, grasps him by the hair to bear him away. The second scene represents St. Nicholas, bringing back the boy, with the cup still in his hands, and restoring him to the astonished father and mother seated at table. The scene is an animated one. The father with both arms embraces his son, and the mother stretches out her arms. A youth in the group, with clasped hands looks to heaven, and a monk, astonished, lifts his arms. Not least of all, a little dog betrays his recognition of the restored boy. [3]

Another story of this kind is thus told in the Golden Legend:

Another nobleman prayed to S. Nicholas that he would, by his merits, get of our Lord that he might have a son, and promised that he would bring his son to the church, and would offer him a cup of gold. Then the son was born and came to age, and the father commanded to make a cup, and the cup pleased him much, and he retained it for himself, and did do make another of the same value. And they went sailing in a ship toward the church of S. Nicholas, and when the child would have filled the cup, he fell into the water with the cup and anon was lost, and came no more up. Yet nevertheless the father performed his avow, in weeping much tenderly for his son; and when he came to the altar of S. Nicholas he offered the second cup, and when he had offered it, it fell down, like as one had cast it under the altar. And he took it up and set it again upon the altar, and then yet was it cast further than tofore, and yet he took it up and remised it the third time upon the altar; and it was thrown again further than tofore. Of which thing all they that were there marvelled, and men came for to see this thing. And anon, the child that had fallen in the sea, came again prestly before them all, and brought in his hands the first cup, and recounted to the people that, anon as he was fallen in the sea, the blessed S. Nicholas came and kept him that he had none harm. And thus the father was glad and offered to S. Nicholas both the two cups.

This story is represented in one of the frescoed

Brogi

Fresco at S. Croce, Attributed to G. Starnina. St. Nicholas Restores to his Father the Son with the Cup lost at Sea.

scenes in the Chapel of the Sacrament at Santa Croce in Florence and in the Franciscan Church at Assisi. It also forms one of the scenes carved on the Winchester baptismal font.

Still another story in which St. Nicholas appears as the guardian angel of schoolboys, is the one dealing with the resuscitation of the three schoolboys murdered on their journey home. The story, which appears in a number of variant forms, relates how three boys, on their journey home from school, take lodging at an inn, or as some versions have it, farmhouse. In the night the treacherous host and hostess murder the boys, cut up their three bodies, and throw the pieces into casks used for salting meat. In the morning St. Nicholas. appears and calls the guilty ones to task. They deny guilt, but are convicted when the saint causes the boys, sound of body and limb, to arise from the casks. This story, of repellent detail, is "not known among the Greeks, who are so devoted to St. Nicholas."[4] It is also not included in the Golden Legend nor in the Roman *Breviary*. It seems to have been one of the elements added to the legend after the development of St. Nicholas worship in the West. Its earliest record is said to be that in the French life of St. Nicholas by Wace. With the incident in the story, Wace connects the great honor paid to St. Nicholas by schoolboys. "Because," says Wace, "he did such honor to schoolboys, they celebrate this day [Dec. 6] by reading and singing and reciting the miracles of St. Nicholas."

Different attempts have been made to explain the origin of this, at first, repellent story. One critic finds the explanation of the story in the conventional methods of medieval art. He explains it as growing out of a misinterpretation of an illustration representing one of the incidents in the earlier story of St. Nicholas, the well-known story of the succor lent by St. Nicholas to the three officers condemned to death by Constantine. The three captives, after the manner of the Middle Ages, were supposedly represented in a tower, and in order to make the scene more visible, only the upper part of the tower was represented. Then, too, in order to bring about the desired subordination of human to divine, the medieval artist would reduce the size of tower and prisoners in relation to the intervening saint, so that the tower would become, in appearance, a cask, and the three officers, little boys. From this pictorial representation misunderstood, if we adopt this theory, arose the story of the three boys brought to life from the packing cask.[4]

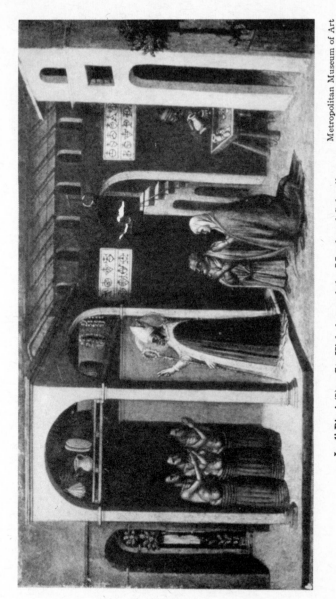

L. di Bicci (?).   St. Nicholas and the Murdered Schoolboys.

Metropolitan Museum of Art

Another explanation of the story is to be found in the association, to be discussed later, between St. Nicholas and the northern water demon known as "Nix" or "Old Nick." According to belief prevalent in northern lands, the souls of drowned people are kept by Nix in pots. When one remembers that souls were generally represented in the form of children, one may see the close analogy between the pots of the water demon and the tubs from which St. Nicholas resuscitated the schoolboys. [5]

Mrs. Jameson has still another explanation to offer. To use her own words: "The story is sometimes treated as a religious allegory, referring to the conversion of sinners or unbelievers. In some pictures the host is represented as a demon with hoofs and claws."

The explanations just offered, afford interesting illustration of the ingenuity of the folk-lorist but seem superfluous. The tale could hardly be improved on for the use it serves, to excite the gratitude of young schoolboys. The details, repellent perhaps to the modern adult, trained in the school of modern naturalism, are, if one stops to think, features characteristic of the world's classic folk-tales for children. The ogre-like ferocity of the host and hostess where the boys lodged, is quite

4

in keeping with the tone of little Red Riding Hood
or of Bluebeard.

In any event we may infer popularity of this
tale from its wide prevalence. The central scene
of the famous story is represented among the
sculptured scenes of the church of St. Nicholas at
Bari, and among the frescoed scenes at Santa
Croce. It is pictured on the pages of the Salis-
bury missal and forms the subject of several
canvas paintings by early artists. Up to within
recent times a picture of St. Nicholas standing by
a tub from which were emerging three boys, was
to be seen painted on the side of a prominent
house in Amsterdam, with the inscription "Sinterklaes." [6] It was one of the stories dramatically
presented by medieval schoolboys on St. Nicholas'
eve. Down to our own day it has continued to
be the subject of a song used in the popular dances
of the Faröe Islands. The youths rising from the
cask became a constant symbol used in representing St. Nicholas. In the churches of Brittany,
and doubtless elsewhere in France and Belgium,
among the images of saints occupying places on
the pillars within the church, or standing as sen-
tinels on each side of the recessed portals, St.
Nicholas is frequently to be met with, always to
be recognized by his conventional pedestal formed

F. Pesellino.   St. Nicholas and the Murdered Schoolboys.

Alinari

by the tub from which are issuing the three saved boys.

A charming version of the story appears in a French folk-song, effectively rendered by Yvette Guilbert appropriately garbed in the robes of the kindly bishop. Anatole France, too, has brought to bear on this story, his gift of paradox in a highly diverting version containing a sequel in which the innocent St. Nicholas suffers every conceivable form of injury from the three rescued boys, who prove to be incarnations of three varied forms of human depravity.

St. Nicholas, the youth of exemplary piety, we may hope inspired proper emulation on the part of schoolboys. St. Nicholas, the generous protector, and friend, we may be sure was an object of schoolboy gratitude and love. The memory of his kindly deeds was kept alive not only in recited story, but in carved stone and painted wall. The boys themselves sang about them in beloved songs and enacted them in spirited plays. But the beneficence of the kindly saint was not confined to the past. The gifts mysteriously bestowed on the saint's festival eve have kept alive the feelings of gratitude, and through the centuries boys have continued to look to St. Nicholas for aid and protection. "St. Nicholas be thy speed," facetiously remarks Launce, to Speed who is about to give an exhibition of his ability to read. Even in his athletics the English schoolboy has continued to invoke the assistance of his patron saint. According to Brand,[7] if a boy is pursued and about to be caught, the cry of *Nic'las* entitles him to a suspension of the play for a moment. Or if he is not ready, or is obliged to stop, to fasten his shoe or make other readjustment, the same magic word affords him protection. One is reluctant to associate St. Nicholas with the methods, not always above question, sometimes used by the athlete in order to gain time or wind, but this continued use of the name of Nicholas in sports bears eloquent testimony to the place their saint has occupied in the hearts of schoolboys.

A. Lorenzetti.   St. Nicholas Providing the Dower for the Three Maidens

CHAPTER IV

ST. NICHOLAS AND THE DOWERLESS MAIDENS

REFERENCE has already been made to the fact that after the introduction of Christianity the name of St. Nicholas came to be associated with a number of customs antedating Christianity and that to some extent, mainly superficially, the earlier customs were influenced by the new association. Thus the gift giving of apples and pears and nuts and of rods to children, characteristic of the pre-Christian autumn festivals, was brought into association with St. Nicholas, probably largely because the pre-Christian festival coincided in time with the time of the St. Nicholas celebration, December sixth. With the transfer of this old custom to the Christmas celebration, the custom of giving gifts to children coalesced with another, an adult custom of gift giving, derived from the Roman *strenæ*, a feature of the Roman celebration of the Kalends of January, and surviving distinctly in Latin countries, notably in the *étrennes* of the French New Year's Day. With both of these customs coalescing in the general gift giving of Christmas, in America at least, is still associated the name of Santa Claus, or St. Nicholas.

Aside from the coincidence in time between the St. Nicholas festival and the pagan children's festival, there was also a point of contact in one of the best-known of the stories in the life of St. Nicholas, which, associated with the earlier custom at first in a superficial way, in time affected its character. The story in question is the famous one of the young man St. Nicholas and his gifts to the dowerless maidens. This story in the condensed, not too lively, version in the Golden Legend, runs as follows:

And when his father and mother were departed out of this life, he [the young man Nicholas] began to think how he might distribute his riches, and not to the praising of the world but to the honor and glory of God. And it was so that one, his neighbour, had then three daughters, virgins, and he was a nobleman: but for the poverty of them together, they were constrained, and in very purpose to abandon them to the sin of lechery, so that by the gain and winning of their infamy they might be sustained. And when the holy man Nicholas knew hereof he had great horror of this villainy, and threw by night secretly into the house of the man a mass of gold wrapped in a

Florentine School (Fifteenth Century). St. Nicholas and the Three Maidens.

cloth. And when the man arose in the morning, he found this mass of gold, and rendered to God therefor great thankings, and therwith he married his oldest daughter. And a little while after this holy hermit of God threw in another mass of gold, which the man found and thanked God, and purposed to wake for to know him that had aided him in his poverty. And after a few days Nicholas doubled the mass of the gold, and cast it into the house of this man. He awoke by the sound of the gold and followed Nicholas, which fled from him, and he said to him: "Sir, flee not away so but that I may see and know thee." Then he ran after him more hastily and knew that it was Nicholas; and anon he kneeled down, and would have kissed his feet, but the holy man would not, but required him not to tell nor discover this thing as long as he lived.

This is the story which in general has linked the name of St. Nicholas particularly with the virtue of generosity. For instance, in Dante's *Purgatorio* the shade of Hugh Capet introduces the name of Nicholas in this connection.

> Esso parlava ancor della largezza
> che fece Niccolao alle pulcelle,
> per condurre ad onor lor giovenezza.

"It spoke further of the generosity of Nicholas toward the maidens in order to conduct their youth to honor."

Canto xx., vo. 31–33.

Among schoolboys the story was particularly
well known. It formed the subject of one of the
plays performed by them on St. Nicholas' eve.
It, also, more frequently than any other incident
in his life story, forms the subject of pictures by
Byzantine and early Italian painters. The pictures representing the dejected father and the
daughters preparing for bed, one of the daughters
sometimes dutifully pulling off her father's boots,
and the youth St. Nicholas on the outside of the
house furtively casting through an open window
his gifts of gold, inevitably bring to mind the
later methods of gift bestowing employed by Santa
Claus. That the connection was felt in earlier
times is made clear from earlier references to the
custom, especially in the form of Protestant
objection. For instance, a preacher of Lauban
in 1608, referring to St. Nicholas' gifts to the
maidens, remarks: "Hence comes the custom that
some parents lay something on the bed for children and say St. Nicholas has given it, which is an
evil custom since by it the children are directed
to St. Nicholas when we know that not St. Nicholas but the holy Christ Child gives us everything
good for body or for soul."[1] Another Protestant
preacher of the same period makes similar objection, saying: "One had better tell the children

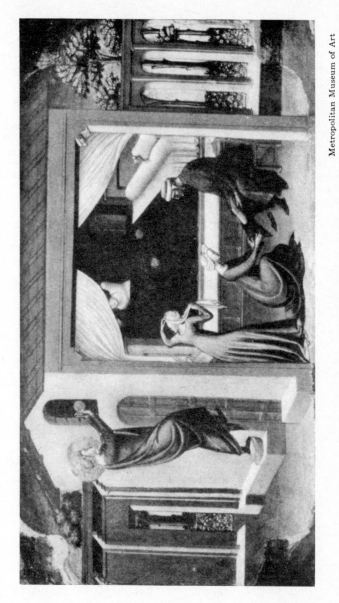

Metropolitan Museum of Art

L. di Bicci (?).   St. Nicholas and the Three Maidens.

that the dear Christ Child sent such gifts; if they shall be good, better ones will follow on Christmas day." The surreptitious manner of conveying the gifts to the children must have been an old practice as may be inferred from the incident recorded of the young man of the sixteenth century who, in attempting to imitate St. Nicholas, fell through an opening left for grain and nearly lost his life.[2]

That the association of St. Nicholas with gift giving was known in England in the sixteenth century, is shown by the following lines from Barnabe Googe's *Popish Kingdom*, a translation from the *Regnum Antichristi* by Naogeorgus:

"Saint Nicholas money used to give to maidens
    secretly.
Who that be still may use his wonted liberality;
The mothers all their children on the eve do cause to
    fast,
And when they every one at night in senseless sleep
    are cast,
Both apples, nuts, and pears they bring, and other
    things beside,
As caps, and shoes and petticoats, with other things
    they hide,
And in the morning found, they say, 'Saint Nicholas
    this brought.'"[3]

Down to within recent times in the church of S. Nicola in Carcere at Rome, the generosity of

St. Nicholas was annually commemorated, by the giving of gifts to poor children in the sacristy after the memorial Mass on St. Nicholas' day. This custom at Rome seems to have been discontinued, but the memory of it, and the attending hopes for gifts, are not extinct, as the present writer had opportunity to observe when attending services in honor of St. Nicholas at this church on St. Nicholas' day, in 1914. After the Mass a throng of expectant parents and children followed the officiating priest into the sacristy and were permitted to kiss the ring on the hand of the officiating priest, but in their hope for the customary presents, met with keenly felt disappointment.

But although in modern times deprived somewhat of the gratitude once felt for him as a giver of gifts, St. Nicholas for centuries has been honored on account of another phase of his kindly art, the procuring of husbands for marriageable girls. Reference has already been made to the fact that in the Netherlands the special cakes of the St. Nicholas festival are said to perpetuate a custom originated by the three daughters in the story, who on their marriage day are said to have baked such cakes and distributed them among poor children as a sign of gratitude.

Honor paid to St. Nicholas by unwedded maids

goes back a great many centuries. Among
Normans of the twelfth century he was regarded
as the peculiar saint of spinsters, who invoked
him in order to procure speedy marriage.[4]

The same idea is in evidence in English popular
carols, in which St. Nicholas is praised particularly as a provider of husbands. One song of
seven stanzas recites the story of how St. Nicholas
saved the maidens, and ends with the stanza:

" Seynt Nicholas, at the townys ende,
 Consoylid the maydens hom to wynde,
 And throw Godes grace he xulde hem synae
 Husbondes thre, good and kind."

The refrain is:

"Alle maydenis for Godes Grace,
 Worchepe ye seynt Nicolas."[5]

One of the most important of marriages in English
history is associated with this St. Nicholas custom.
In one of Bishop Fisher's sermons it is recorded
of Margaret, Countess of Richmond, mother of
Henry VII., "that she prayed to St. Nicholas,
the patron and helper of all true maydens, when
nine years old, about the choice of a husband;
and that the saint appeared to her in a vision and
announced the Earl of Richmond."[6]

From another ancient authority we have similar testimony,[7] as follows:

St. Nicholas was likewise venerated as the protector of virgins; there are, or were until lately, numerous fantastical customs observed in Italy and various parts of France, in reference to that peculiar tutelary personage. In several convents it was customary, on the eve of St. Nicholas for the boarders (*sic*) to place each a silk stocking at the door of the apartment of the abbess with a piece of paper enclosed, recommending themselves to "great St. Nicholas of her chamber," and the next day they were called together to witness the saint's attention, who never failed to fill the stockings with sweetmeats and other trifles of that kind, with which these credulous virgins made a general feast.

If the kindly saint, in this case, was not in position to provide husbands, he at least provided agreeable consolation.

The conception of St. Nicholas as the protector of maidens and the provider of husbands and the association of this idea with the story of his generous act toward the three maidens in distress, is by no means extinct in our own times, as is shown by the following account of English customs recorded in a recent newspaper:[8]

In the mining districts of the North of England

L. di Bicci.   Madonna and Child and Various Saints with their Conventional Emblems.

they still maintain the pleasant custom of collecting "maidens' purses" on Christmas eve.

These purses, in most cases subscribed for by the mining folk themselves, are intended as marriage portions for girls undowered with worldly wealth, who are expecting to be led to the altar. On Christmas eve the full purse is stealthily thrown in at the girl's window to avoid any possibility of wounding her feelings.

In one parish four purses are provided every Christmas eve by a woman now rich, who makes no secret of the fact that her own wedding day was brightened by the gift thrown in at the window when she was a miner's lass.

Among the images of saints in France and other northern countries of Europe, as has already been remarked, the tub with the three saved youths is the conventional sign of St. Nicholas. Italian artists, on the other hand, represent St. Nicholas in bishop's garb and with three golden balls, commonly on a book which he holds in his hand, but sometimes in his cap or at his feet.[9] This conventional symbol of the three balls is sometimes explained as alluding to the Trinity, or to the loaves of bread used by the saint in feeding the poor in a famine, but is more usually associated with the three gifts to the three maidens, the balls of gold corresponding in appearance to the handfuls of gold tied up in a handkerchief thrown in at the window by St. Nicholas, in the representations of the scene.

Remote as at first thought may appear the connection between St. Nicholas and pawnbrokers, it seems possible also to connect the three balls, the conventional sign for St. Nicholas, with the more modern use of the three balls as the sign of the professional money-lender. The pawnbroker's three balls have been sometimes explained as derived from the arms of the Medici. A more generally received explanation is that the three balls were used as a sign before their houses by the Lombard bankers. "The three blue balls," says Brand,[10] "prefixed to the doors and windows of pawnbrokers' shops (by the vulgar humorously enough said to indicate that it is *two to one* that the things are ever redeemed) were in reality *the arms of a set of merchants from Lombardy*, who were the first that publicly lent money on pledges. They dwelt together on a street from them called Lombard Street, in London." It has been said that "the golden balls were originally three flat yellow effigies of byzants, or gold coins, laid heraldically upon a sable field, but that they were presently converted into balls the better to attract attention."[11]

A plausible explanation, which, however, remains

to be proved, would be found in the association of the three balls of the pawnbroker with the three golden balls, the symbol of St. Nicholas, whom the Lombard bankers might well have chosen as their patron saint. If one were disposed to be uncharitable, one might call attention to the fact that St. Nicholas was the patron saint not only of schoolboys and unwedded maids, and as remains to be shown, of mariners, but also of pirates and thieves, between whom and the kindly saint the connection is not, at first thought, obvious, and one might try to show a relationship between the pawnbroker who lends money on pledges, and the pirate or thief who borrows money without a pledge. The suggestion is not intended seriously, but it is seriously believed that the association with St. Nicholas is not more unlikely in one case than in the other. Confirmatory evidence is afforded by the legend of the saint, in which is included an episode that seems to establish St. Nicholas as the protector of the money-lender as firmly as the stories already discussed associate him with the protection of boys and of maidens. In the Golden Legend the story is told as follows:

There was a man that had borrowed of a Jew a sum of money, and sware upon the altar of St. Nicholas that he would render and pay it again as soon as he might, and gave none other pledge. And this man held this money so long, that the Jew demanded and asked his money, and he said that he had paid him. Then the Jew made him to come before the law in judgment, and the oath was given to the debtor. And he brought with him an hollow staff, in which he had put the money in gold, and he leant upon the staff. And when he should make his oath and swear, he delivered his staff to the Jew to keep and hold whilst he should swear, and then sware that he had delivered more than he ought to him. And when he had made the oath, he demanded his staff again of the Jew, and he nothing knowing of his malice, delivered it to him. Then this deceiver went his way, and anon after, him list sore to sleep, and laid him in the way, and a cart with four wheels came with great force and slew him, and broke the staff with gold that it spread abroad. And when the Jew heard this, he came thither sore moved, and saw the fraud, and many said to him that he should take to him the gold; and he refused it, saying, But if he that was dead were not raised again to life by the merits of St. Nicholas, he would not receive it, and if he came again to life, he would receive baptism and become Christian. Then he that was dead arose, and the Jew was christened.

This story forms the subject of three spirited scenes in the frescoes at Santa Croce, which represent the borrowing of the money, the oath on the book before the altar of St. Nicholas, a place detail neglected in the Golden Legend version,

Fresco at S. Croce, Attributed to G. Starnina. Three Scenes from the Story of St. Nicholas and the Jew
Moneylender.

and the street scene where the sharper is run over.

The singular reversal of the rôle usually assigned to the Jew in medieval story is striking. The main purpose of the story seems to be not so much to show the lack of appreciation on the part of St. Nicholas of the sharp trick played, the kind of trick that medieval story loved to record, especially when a Jew was the sufferer by the chicanery, as to show the justice of St. Nicholas and perhaps, if we are disposed to be skeptical about the truth of the story, owes its origin to the desire to establish a relation of protectorship between St. Nicholas and the money-lending class, as other stories established him as the protector of schoolboys, of maidens, and of mariners.

Another of the best known stories of St. Nicholas, which tells of the protection afforded a Jew on another occasion, remains to be recorded in another connection.[12] In any event there seems to be good evidence in the story of St. Nicholas for associating the three balls, his conventional sign, with the three balls of the pawnbroker, and thus establishing a connection, at first thought so far-fetched, between the pawnbroker class and the story of the dowerless maids.

CHAPTER V

THE BOY BISHOP, OR NICHOLAS BISHOP

IN all the representations of St. Nicholas, painting or image, except those pictures dealing
with his childhood, he appears with the robes and
insignia of a bishop. St. Nicholas is preëminently
the bishop-saint. Concerning his boyhood elevation to the episcopal rank, legend has an interesting story to relate. Once more let us turn to the
Golden Legend, which relates the story as follows:

After this the bishop of Mirea died and other bishops
assembled for to purvey to this church a bishop. And
there was, among the others, a bishop of great authority, and all the election was in him. And when he had
warned all for to be in fastings and in prayers, this
bishop heard that night a voice which said to him that,
at the hour of matins, he should take heed to the doors
of the church, and him that should come first to the
church, and have the name of Nicholas they should
sacre him bishop. And he showed this to the other
bishops and admonished them for to be all in prayers;
and he kept the doors. And this was a marvelous
thing, for at the hour of matins, like as he had been

sent from God, Nicholas arose tofore all other. And
the bishop took him when he was come and demanded
of him his name. And he, which was simple as a dove,
inclined his head, and said: I have to name Nicholas.
Then the bishop said to him: Nicholas, Servant and
friend of God, for your holiness ye shall be bishop of
this place. And sith they brought him to the church,
howbeit that he refused it strongly, yet they set him
in the chair. And he followed, as he did tofore in all
things, in humility and honesty of manners. He
woke in prayer and made his body lean, he eschewed
company of women, he was humble in receiving all
things, profitable in speaking, joyous in admonishing,
and cruel in correcting.

This episode is the most celebrated in the life of
St. Nicholas. It is represented in a number of
Italian paintings. The early morning appearance
of the boy Nicholas at the church and his surprise
as he learns of his election are presented in particularly lively manner in one of the scenes from his
life by Lorenzetti preserved at Florence.[1]

Interesting in itself, the story of the elevation
of the boy Nicholas to the rank of bishop also
possesses interest because associated with some of
the most interesting of early church customs, those
centering about the personage of the Boy Bishop,
or Nicholas Bishop as he was sometimes called.
The explanation of this interesting personage and
the customs associated with him, like that of

Santa Claus, is a complex one. In the case of the Boy Bishop customs once more we have probably to do with the survival of pre-Christian customs with which the Church associated new names and new meaning.

The spirit that dominated the Christian December celebration and many details of the external form of celebration are to be found in the Roman pagan customs of December and early January. The early winter season in Roman times was a period of general relaxation and merry making. In the week beginning December 17th and ending December 23d, the ancient god Saturn resumed once more, for a limited period, the benign rule of which he had been deprived by his more strenuous, shall we say more efficient, son Jove. The week of the rule of Saturn, the *Saturnalia*, was a time of revelry and riot. The serious was barred. No business was allowed; drinking and games and noise prevailed. All men were to be equal, rich and poor, slave and free. There was chosen a mock king who could impose forfeits. The Roman New Year's feast had a similar character. As at the *Saturnalia*, masters drank and gambled with slaves.[2] In the words of the Greek sophist, Libanius: "From the minds of young people it (the New Year's feast) removes

A. Lorenzetti. The Boy Nicholas Indicated as the Divine Choice for Bishop.

two kinds of dread: the dread of the schoolmaster and the dread of the stern pedagogue."

The attitude of the Christian church toward pagan custom is well known. Since it could not hope to extirpate old practice, it endeavored to adapt it to Christian use, giving to it Christian meaning and, as far as possible, Christian character. It aimed to make the birth of Christ, and the associated events, the dominating idea in its celebration at the beginning of winter. In spite of this intention, in the popular customs of the Christmas season, even in the ceremonies of the Church, there is apparent a survival of many features of pagan practice. Especially in the practice of the week following Christmas, there is to be observed the leveling or inversion of rank, the election of a mock ruler, and the general relaxation of discipline that were features of the pagan celebrations of the same season at Rome. Thus in the three days immediately following Christmas, church discipline was sufficiently relaxed to permit of revels in turn, by the lower orders of clergy and by the choir boys. December 26th, St. Stephen's day, was the day for the deacons, since St. Stephen was a deacon. For this day the deacons supplanted the higher dignitaries and took the preëminence in the divine services. On

Christmas night, the eve of St. Stephen's day, after vespers, the deacons formed a pompous procession dressed in silk copes like priests. On St. Stephen's day the deacons performed the parts of the divine service. There was also a great deal of mock ceremonial, and drinking and processions in the streets, with visiting of houses and levying of contributions.[3] On the following day, the day of St. John the Evangelist, the priests had their innings. Features of their celebration were mock blessings and the proclamation of a ribald form of indulgence. On the eve of Innocents' day (Dec. 28th), the priests gave way to the choir boys, "the children," for the celebration of Childermas. On Circumcision Day (Jan. 1st), the sub-deacons, the "rookies" among the priestly orders, took their turn at occupying the places of the higher clergy.

The day of the sub-deacons, possibly because of its coincidence with the Roman Kalends, was celebrated in a particularly mad fashion. In the words "*Deposuit potentes de sede: et exaltavit humiles*" sung in the *Magnificat* at Vespers, was found the suggestion for a general inversion in rank. For the time, the places of rank and honor were taken by the lowly sub-deacons. The sacred services were burlesqued in most shocking fashion varying

in different places. In Paris[4] in the fifteenth
century, "priests danced in the choir dressed as
women, panders, or minstrels. Wanton songs
were sung. Black puddings were eaten at the
horn of the altar while mass was being celebrated,
and the altar was censed with ashes or by the
smoke from the soles of old shoes." Performers
without the church were even more irreverent
and riotous in character.

The choir boy customs of Holy Innocents' day
were somewhat like those described, although
more restrained in character, since, as Mr. Chambers has remarked, boys were more amenable
to discipline than the older clergy. There was a
similar inversion of rank and, within limit, a
similar burlesque of custom, on this day the choir
boys taking precedence in rank, presided over by
one of their number, usually elected on St. Nicholas' day, with the title of Boy Bishop, or Nicholas
Bishop.

A central feature of the celebration was a pompous church procession following vespers on
Childermas eve. In this procession the inversion
of rank was a feature. The book, the censer, and
the candles, usually borne by boys, on this occasion were borne by reverend canons, and when
at the end of the ceremony the procession re-

turned to the choir, the boys took the places of
dignity in the higher stalls, with the Boy Bishop
in the stall of the bishop or dean.   Then followed
a feature doubtless in the estimation of the boys
not less important than the procession, namely a
supper provided by one of the church dignitaries.

On Innocents' day all the services, including the
Mass, were performed by the boys with their
"Bishop," also in many places the "Bishop"
preached a sermon.   Nor were the honor and
dignity of the Boy Bishop confined to the ceremonies within the church.   In mounted procession, with attendant boy prebends, he visited other
religious houses and houses of neighboring people
of prominence, singing songs and imparting blessings in the expectation of festal entertainment and
of money gifts as well.   In the year 1555 the "chylde
byshope" of St. Paul's with his company visited
Queen Mary at St. James's and sang a song before her both on St. Nicholas' day (Dec. 6th) and
on Innocents' day (Dec. 28th).   The amounts
collected on these occasions were considerable.
Robert de Holme,[5] who was "Bishop" at York,
received from the choirmaster, who served as
treasurer, in 1369, the sum of £3 15s. 1½ d.   But
this was only a part of the receipts, for at in-
tervals during the fortnight following Christmas,

the "Bishop" with his troupe made trips in the
neighborhood which netted handsome profit, the
countess of Northumberland alone contributing
twenty shillings and a gold ring.[6] In Aberdeen
the master of the grammar school was paid by a
collection taken when he went the rounds with the
"Bishop." That this source of revenue was not a
matter of trivial importance may be inferred from
the interesting statement in the municipal registers
that "he hes na uder fee to leif on."

Some interesting details regarding French ob-
servance of the Boy Bishop custom have been
garnered by Mr. Chambers from the records for
Toul. At that place

the expenses of the feast, with the exception of the
dinner on the day after Innocents' day, which came
out of the disciplinary fines, are assigned by the
statutes to the canons in the order of their appoint-
ment. The responsible canon must give a supper on
Innocents' day, and on the following day a dessert
out of what is over. He must also provide the
"Bishop" with a horse, gloves, and a *biretta* when he
rides abroad. At the supper a curious ceremony took
place. The canon returned thanks to the "Bishop,"
apologized for any shortcomings in the preparations,
and finally handed the "Bishop" a cap of rosemary
or other flowers, which was then conferred upon the
canon to whose lot it would fall to provide the feast
for the next anniversary. Should the canon disregard

his duties the boys and sub-deacons were entitled to
hang up a black cope on a candlestick in the middle
of the choir *in illius vituperium* for as long as they
might choose.

The elaborateness, too, of the manner of celebration, as well as the constant association with
St. Nicholas, may be inferred from the following
Northumberland inventory of robes and ornaments
belonging to one of these Boy Bishops:[7]

Imprimis, i. myter, well garnished with perle and
precious stones, with nowches of silver and gilt before
and behind. Item, iiii. rynges of silver and gilt,
with four ridde precious stones in them. Item, i.
pontifical with silver and gilt, with a blue stone in
hytt. Item, i. owche, broken, silver and gilt, with
iiii. precious stones, and a perle in the mydds. Item,
a croose, with a staff of coper and gilt, with the ymage
of St. Nicolas in the mydds. Item, i. vestment,
redde, with lyons, with silver, with brydds of gold in
the orferes of the same. Item, i. albe to the same, with
starres in the paro. Item, i. white cope, stayned
with tristells and orferes, redde sylke, with does of
gold, and whytt napkins about the necks. Item,
iiii. copes, blew sylk with red orferes, trayled, with
whitt braunchis and flowers. Item, i. steyned cloth
of the ymage of St. Nicholas. Item, i. taberd of
skarlet, and a hodde thereto lyned with whitt sylk.
Item, a hode of skarlett, lyned with blue sylk.

The earliest known reference to the Boy Bishop

custom is from St. Gall in the year 911. King
Conrad I. was visiting Bishop Solomon of Con-
stance and heard so much of the Vespers procession at St. Gall that he determined to visit the
monastery at the time of the revels. He found it
"all very amusing and especially the procession
of children, so grave and sedate that even when
Conrad bade his train roll apples along the aisle,
they did not budge."[8] In later years the custom
lost much of its early sobriety, although doubtless
a great deal of dignity, real or assumed, persisted
in the church procession. The custom pervaded
most of the countries of Europe in the following
centuries.

In France it was not abolished until 1721. At
Mainz, in Germany, it was not wholly extinct in
1779.[9] In Belgium in the nineteenth century
there survived a number of popular customs showing for the celebration of Innocents' day of the
present the same kind of inversion of authority
that characterized the Boy Bishop customs of
earlier times. Innocents' day is in Belgium more
than in other countries a popular festival, making
up somewhat for the fact that in Belgium, Christmas is less of a children's celebration than in other
Teutonic countries, or perhaps owing to the greater
importance of St. Nicholas customs in the Nether-

lands than in other countries. In any event, in
Belgium, Innocents' day is a real children's festival: children are masters in the house, and parents must obey them. At Antwerp, in Brabant.
and in some parts of the county of Limbourg,
little boys and girls dress up for the day as papas
and mammas. Usually the youngest of the family
receives the key to the pantry and orders in the
kitchen the meals for the day.[10]

In England the Boy Bishop custom, which
came to an end in the sixteenth century under
Reformation influence, once prevailed throughout
the length and breadth of the land—at first in
cathedrals, collegiate churches, and schools, later
"in every parish church where there was a suffi-
cient band of choristers to furnish forth the
Boy Bishop ceremonial, or sufficiently well-to-
do parishioners to be worth laying under contribution."[11]

The relation of the Boy Bishop to St. Nicholas
customs offers a number of difficulties to explain.
Mr. Chambers leans to the view that the custom
was originally associated with St. Nicholas' day,
an opinion supported by the fact that the "Bishop"
was elected on the eve of St. Nicholas. But he
believes that, like other St. Nicholas customs,
the Santa Claus custom for instance, it was later

transferred to the Christmas season. Something, however, may be said for a contrary explanation. It is an established fact that medieval schools and universities had their origin in the song schools of the Church; consequently in schools and universities there survived customs originally appropriate only to choir boys. In this way might be transferred a custom observed by choir boys on the festival at Holy Innocents' day (Dec. 28th), to St. Nicholas' day (Dec. 6th), the festival day of schoolboys, and the Boy Bishop of Innocents' day get the name of *Episcopus Nicholatensis*, "Nicholas Bishop," or by an admirable Latin pun at Eton, "*Episcopus Nihilensis*," "Bishop of Nothing." There is evident relationship between the custom of the Boy Bishop and the story of St. Nicholas elected bishop when a boy. Did the custom grow out of the story, or as is so often the case, did the story originate as an explanation of an established custom?

Oliver Wendell Holmes, on the occasion of a visit paid, late in life, to Westminster Abbey, singles out from "amidst all the imposing recollections of the ancient edifice," one that impressed him "in the inverse ratio of its importance, . . . the little holes in the stones, in one place, where the boys of the choir used to play marbles." In a similar way it may be remarked that among all the magnificent ceremonies in the history of the Church, few are more impressive than those associated with the Boy Bishop, or Nicholas Bishop. The choir boy, exercising his rule over his fellow boys, riding with them in parade about the city or surrounding country, or for the nonce lording it over his pompous superiors and indulging in playful parody of the ceremonies in which throughout the year he has taken a not always too patient part,—all this affords us a glimpse at natural boy nature centuries ago.

CHAPTER VI

IT will have been noted that St. Nicholas is not
only the patron saint of youths, but is himself
a youthful saint. His most distinctive deeds, at
least the deeds about the memory of which have
most been interwoven popular customs, are deeds
performed by him as a young man. The distinctive feature about his election as bishop was that
he was elected when a mere youth. But before
his election as bishop he had already distinguished
himself by his act of generosity in saving the three
daughters of the impoverished nobleman. Also,
according to the account of his life in the Roman
Breviary, the act upon which is based his reputation as protector of seamen was accomplished by
him as a young man when on a pious pilgrimage,
on the return from which he was miraculously
directed to Myra, there to be chosen bishop. In
a way, then, the election as bishop forms a kind of
climax to a series of youthful accomplishments.

But the life story of St. Nicholas differs from the typical saint's legend in that it is not the record of one single achievement that absorbed all the energies of the story's hero and whose accomplishment formed a dramatic close. On the contrary, as already remarked, his legend is made up of a series of beneficent acts, in part accomplished by the living saint, in part accomplished by him after death serving as a protecting spirit. Besides the youthful deeds already discussed, there remain to be recorded a number of others, some of them hardly less well known than the ones already considered, others not so widely known but of interest, not only in themselves, but as revealing the varied aspects of the kindness of St. Nicholas and showing the enduring character of his fame.

First there remain in the Golden Legend two well known stories that deserve to be included here. One of these, in which St. Nicholas accomplished an ultra-modern function, that of "Food Comptroller," will make clear why he was popular as the patron saint of cities. The story goes:

It was so on a time that all the province of S. Nicolas suffered great famine, in such wise that victual failed. And then this holy man heard say that certain ships laden with wheat were arrived in the

A. Lorenzetti.   St. Nicholas Saving a City in Time of Famine.

haven. And anon he went thither and prayed the
mariners that they would succor the perished at
least with an hundred muyes of wheat of every ship.
And they said: Father, we dare not, for it is meted and
measured, and we must give reckoning thereof in
the garners of the emperor in Alexandria. And the
holy man said to them: Do this that I have said to
you, and I promise, in the truth of God, that it shall
not be lessened or minished when ye shall come to
the garners. And when they had delivered so much
out of every ship, they came into Alexandria and
delivered the measure that they had received. And
then they recounted the miracle to the ministers of
the emperor, and worshiped and praised strongly
God and his servant Nicholas. Then the holy man
distributed the wheat to every man after that he had
need, in such wise that it sufficed for two years, not
only for to sell, but also to sow.

The art of the early Italian painters in handling
narrative subjects is once more admirably illustrated in the animated presentation of this story
in the paintings by Lorenzetti and by Fra Angelico.

In another of the stories included in the Golden
Legend, St. Nicholas twice appears in his favorite
rôle as the protector of human life. The story,
with double catastrophe, goes as follows:

And in this time certain men rebelled against the
emperor; and the emperor sent against them three
princes, Nepotian, Ursyn, and Apollyn. And they
came into the port Adriatic for the wind, which was

6

contrary to them; and the blessed Nicholas commanded
them to dine with him, for he would keep his people
from the ravin that they made. And whilst they
were at dinner, the consul, corrupt by money, had
commanded three innocent knights to be beheaded.
And when the blessed Nicholas knew this, he prayed
these three princes that they would much hastily go
with him. And when they were come where they
should be beheaded, he found them on their knees,
and blindfold, and the righter brandished his sword
over their heads. Then S. Nicholas, embraced with the
love of God, set him hardily against the righter, and
took the sword out of his hand, and threw it from him,
and unbound the innocents, and led them with him
all safe. And anon he went to the judgment to the
consul, and found the gates closed, which anon he
opened by force. And the consul came anon and
saluted him: and this holy man having this saluta-
tion in despite, said to him: Thou enemy of God,
corrupter of the law, wherefore hast thou consented
to so great evil and felony, how darest thou look on
us? And when he had sore chidden and reproved
him, he repented, and at the prayer of the three princes
he received him to penance. After, when the mes-
sengers of the emperor had received his benediction,
they made their gear ready and departed, and sub-
dued their enemies to the empire without shedding
blood, and sith returned to the emperor, and were
worshipfully received. And after this it happed
that some other in the emperor's house had envy on
the weal of these three princes, and accused them to
the emperor of high treason, and did so much by
prayer and by gifts that they caused the emperor
to be so full of ire that he commanded them to prison,

and without other demand, he commanded that they should be slain that same night. And when they knew it by their keeper, they rent their clothes and wept bitterly; and then Nepotian remembered him how S. Nicholas had delivered the three innocents, and admonested the others that they should require his aid and help. And thus as they prayed S. Nicholas appeared to them and after appeared to Constantine, the emperor, and said to him: Wherefore hast thou taken these three princes with so great wrong, and hast judged them to death without trespass? Arise up hastily, and command that they be not executed, or I shall pray to God that he move battle against thee, in which thou shalt be overthrown, and shalt be made meat to beasts. And the emperor demanded: What art thou that art entered by night into my palace and durst say to me such words? And he said to him: I am Nicholas, bishop of Mirea. And in like wise he appeared to the provost, and feared him, saying with a fearful voice: Thou that hast lost mind and wit, wherefore hast thou consented to the death of innocents? Go forth anon and do thy part to deliver them, or else thy body shall rot, and be eaten with worms, and thy meiny shall be destroyed. And he asked him: Who art thou that so menacest me? And he answered: Know thou that I am Nicholas, the bishop of the city of Mirea. Then that one awoke that other, and each told to other their dreams, and anon sent for them that were in prison, to whom the emperor said: What art magic or sorcery can ye, that ye have this night by illusion caused us to have such dreams? And they said that they were none enchanters ne knew no witchcraft, and also that they had not deserved the sentence of death. Then the emperor said to them: Know ye well a man named Nicholas? And when they heard speak of the name of the holy saint, they held up their hands toward heaven, and prayed our Lord that by the merits of S. Nicholas they might be delivered of this present peril. And when the emperor had heard of them the life and miracles of S. Nicholas, he said to them: Go ye forth, and yield ye thankings to God, which hath delivered you by the prayer of this holy man, and worship ye him; and bear ye to him of your jewels, and pray ye him that he threaten me no more, but that he pray for me and for my realm unto our Lord. And a while after, the said princes went unto the holy man, and fell down on their knees humbly at his feet, saying: Verily thou art the sergeant of God, and the very worshipper and lover of Jesu Christ. And when they had all told this said thing by order, he lift up his hands to heaven and gave thankings and praisings to God, and sent again the princes, well informed, into their countries.

This story, although, so far as known, it does not form the subject of any of the St. Nicholas plays presented by medieval schoolboys, certainly possesses dramatic quality. The first intervention by the protecting saint provides suspense like that before the arrival of a reprieve on the stroke of twelve in a modern melodrama. The scene is strikingly presented in one of the Santa Croce frescoes. One of the young men is represented kneeling blindfolded awaiting the death stroke.

Norman Baptismal Font at Winchester Cathedral, with Sculptured Scenes from the Life of St. Nicholas.

The executioner holds his sword lifted, while St. Nicholas from behind grasps it by the point.

Also both this scene and the second scene in the story are represented in the celebrated Giottesque frescoes at Assisi. In the second scene there is represented a hall with straight ceiling supported by slender columns. In this hall the Emperor Constantine is lying asleep. Nicholas with uplifted hands approaches and commands him to free the three imprisoned princes. The latter, one sees below, behind a barred window, before which stands a great wooden cage.[1]

The twelfth-century life of St. Nicholas by Wace, written, as the reader is told in the opening lines, for the sake of the unlettered, to explain to them the purpose of the St. Nicholas festival newly instituted in the West, contains a number of episodes not included in the more or less official account in the Golden Legend. There is one story which seems like a variant version of that of the three murdered schoolboys, which itself is also included by Wace.[2] A merchant is on his way to visit the saint. On the journey he takes lodgings at an inn and in the night is murdered by the treacherous landlord. His body is cut to pieces and packed in a cask and salted like edible flesh. In the night St. Nicholas restores the merchant to life with his body entirely sound. In the morning the merchant appears, naturally to the astonishment of the landlord, who confesses and worships St. Nicholas.

Wace also includes a short story of how St. Nicholas freed a child possessed by the devil,[3] and still another incident, one more than usually filled with human interest, recorded in connection with the election of St. Nicholas as bishop. The story goes that the hostess at an inn where the youthful bishop-elect had stayed, was so overjoyed at the election, that she left her baby in a bath pan by the fire. In her absence the water boiled. The mother returned in fright but found her child safe and happy.

St. Nicholas in origin was an Oriental saint. In the Eastern Church at the present day his worship is more active than in western Europe. In countries like Greece of to-day there survive the conditions amid which St. Nicholas worship had its origin and amid which legendary stories of him were propagated. His ability to work miracles is still believed in by many a Greek peasant. The following remarkably circumstantial account of an incident supposed to have taken place on May 25, 1909, will illustrate the faith in the goodness and

F. Pesellino.   St. Nicholas Saves the Knights about to be Beheaded.

power of St. Nicholas still alive in certain parts
of Greece.[4]

In a romantic situation, one quarter of an hour
from the village of Sparta in Elis, stands a fine monastery dedicated to St. Nicholas. Every year on the
10th of May—the anniversary of the finding of the
saint's ikon—there come to the monastery thousands
of worshipers from all parts of the Peloponnese, who
bring various offerings to the saint and remain several
days in the romantic monastery, worshiping the
wonder-working ikon and celebrating the annual
festival.

Amongst this year's worshipers was a peasant,
John Doulos, from the village of Bezaïté, who invoked
the help of the saint on behalf of Kyriakula, his young
daughter, who was blind. He brought her to worship at the shrine. The unfortunate girl had lost
her sight on Easter day, when she thought she saw a
great fire before her eyes and fell to the ground. From
that moment she could see nothing. All medical
skill was of no avail, and the despairing Doulos determined to take his daughter to the saint. They
arrived at the monastery on the Wednesday before
the festival. Thursday and Friday, days and nights,
they spent inside the church kneeling before the ikon
in prayer and supplication. Suddenly about dawn
on the Saturday, when the worshipers in the church
were numerous, Kyriakula arose, and crossing herself,
cried:

"Father, father, I see! There are the saint's
candles! There is the ikon!"

A thrill of emotion ran through those present, and

all joined with the girl, whose sight had been restored, in worshiping the ikon of the wonder-working saint. After remaining many hours to bless the name of the saint, the healed girl left the church with her father and joined in the festival. Then she returned to her village, and her restored eyesight told better than words the saint's miracle.

CHAPTER VII

ST. NICHOLAS PLAYS

IN our time the celebration of St. Nicholas' day
has lost much of the ceremony that was once
associated with it. Even in countries like Belgium and Holland, where the day is a great folk
festival, there is little to connect the day with the
story of the beloved bishop-saint. "Sinterklaes"
is better known than St. Nicholas. In early days
the case was different. Particularly in the centuries immediately following the transfer of the
St. Nicholas relics to Italy, the time when the
vogue of the eastern saint reached its height in
the countries of western Europe, in many ways
his story was kept fresh in the popular memory.
Not only did the Boy Bishop custom commemorate,
in somewhat extravagant fashion to be sure, the
elevation of the boy Nicholas to the rank of bishop,
but stories of the life of the saint formed an important part of the *lectiones*, or "readings," for the
day in the church; and more important still, some

of the principal episodes in his life formed the subject, in church schools, for hymns which later developed into little plays.[1]　In the election of the Boy Bishop was reënacted with a great deal of adventitious detail one of these episodes.　In more strictly dramatic fashion were reënacted the four episodes: (1) of the maidens saved from a life of shame; (2) the three murdered schoolboys restored to life; (3) the kidnapped boy restored to his parents; and (4) the Jew that put his treasures in charge of the image of St. Nicholas.

These little St. Nicholas plays have genuine significance in the early history of the modern drama.　At a time when the classical drama was dead, when the works of Plautus and Terence were valued as repositories of sententious expressions and their dramatic character apparently not suspected, when the names tragedy and comedy were almost entirely dissociated from dramatic meaning, by one of the strange ironies of life, under the auspices of the Church, which had been hostile in its attitude toward earlier drama, there was created, seemingly without being realized, the germ from which developed the modern drama. The St. Nicholas plays go back to an early stage in the new dramatic development.　Little dramatic scenes from scriptural story began to find a place in the liturgy of the Church as early as the tenth century. St. Nicholas plays are not much later, and are the earliest ones handling scenes drawn from outside the biblical story. They begin not later than the first of the twelfth century. St. Nicholas may almost be regarded as the patron saint of the modern drama, since he seems to have watched over its birth.

The St. Nicholas plays were represented apparently by the choir boys in connection with the celebration of the festival of their patron saint. The language used was Latin, of a schoolboy variety, but vernacular elements soon began to appear. Forming, as they did, a part of the school service, and presented, as they were, by choir boys, as might be expected, they were for the most part sung or chanted. Their purpose to provide entertainment and their dissociation from the older drama are indicated by the names applied to these primitive dramas. *Miracula* was the name given them when the subject-matter was in mind; when their character and purpose were in mind the name applied to them in Latin was *ludus*, in French, *jeu*. The actors at a comparatively early time in English were called players before the word 'play' had yet acquired its later definitely dramatic meaning.

The subjects from the St. Nicholas story used in these little plays have been mentioned. One should notice what a range of interest is comprised in these four stories. They afford opportunity for the use of many of the cant phrases of the modern dramatic critic. There was a melodrama of crime, a primitive detective play, with St. Nicholas playing the part of detective in discovering the crime of the innkeeper and his wife. There was a play dealing with the rough road to matrimony, ending in a triple marriage, hardly surpassed in modern love comedy. There was a sentimental comedy, with gripping heart interest, in the story of the boy abducted and restored. There was a screaming farce in the story of the Jew that was robbed. It should be noted, too, that the modern "tired business man" would find the endings in all four as happy as could be wished.

One of the early St. Nicholas plays also is of interest because it is one of three plays composed by the earliest determinable personality in connection with the authorship of modern drama. The name of the author, Hilarius, seems to have been no misnomer. He was probably an Englishman,[2] or an Anglo-Norman, who went to France to study under Abélard. He is the author of a number of innocent love poems, playful in tone, addressed to an English Rose and to his nun friends, Bona and Superba. From his writings we learn that he was not only lively, but fat. Along with a number of other students, on account of some misbehavior, he seems to have suffered a kind of rustication and been obliged to leave the monastery where he was studying and to take up residence in a neighboring village. In a mock elegy he feigns despair at being deprived of the privilege of hearing lectures. Altogether the character of this medieval student is easy to associate with the farcical little Latin play which he wrote, back in the twelfth century, presenting the story of the Jew who committed his valuables to the care of the image of St. Nicholas.

This play,[3] or operetta, for it was intended for song and chant by the choir boys, is composed in rimed Latin stanzas, practically impossible to reproduce in form and in spirit with any degree of literalness in English, although Professor Gayley has accomplished the miraculous with one or two of them.

The *dramatis personæ* in the play are: Barbarus (a Heathen), owner of the treasure, corresponding to the Jew in the Golden Legend version of the story, four or six robbers, and St. Nicholas. At first the Heathen, having assembled his treasures, approaches an image of St. Nicholas (represented by a man standing in a shrine) and puts them in care of the image, saying (probably in song):

" Nicolæ, quidquid possideo,
    hoc in meo misi teloneo;
    te custodem rebus adhibeo;
       serva quæ sunt ibi:
    meis, precor, attende precibus;
    vide, nullus sit locus furibus!
    Pretiosis aurum cum vestibus
       ego trado tibi."

The thought of which may be rendered freely:

Nicholas, all that I possess, I have put in this chest. I leave it to you in charge; keep what is here. I pray you, listen to my request. See to it that no thief gets in. I am putting in your charge gold and precious raiment.

In a second like stanza Barbarus expresses the security that he feels now that his valuables are in the charge of the image of St. Nicholas and at the same time warns the image that there will be trouble if anything happens to his property.

When Barbarus has gone, tramps, noticing the house open and without guardian, carry off everything. When Barbarus returns, he finds his treasure gone and expresses his feelings in song. His song consists of three Latin stanzas, each with

a French refrain probably joined in by the other
members of the boy choir.   It begins:

> " Gravis sors et dura!
>   Hic reliqui plura,
>   sed sub mala cura;
>   Des! quel domage!
>   qui pert la sue chose, purque n'enrage? "

The rime scheme of which may be reproduced
something like this:

> Hard luck and sad!
> I left all I had,
> But the care was bad.
>   Gad, what a shame!
> If I am mad, I'm not to blame.

Two stanzas with the same refrain follow.   Then
Barbarus turns to the image and lays on it the
blame in two additional stanzas with the threaten-
ing French refrain:

> " Ha! Nicholax,
>   se ne me rent ma chose, tu ol comparras."

(If you don't give me back my things, I'll make
you pay for it.)

Barbarus then takes up a whip and vents his
feelings in two additional stanzas of the same sort,
the form and spirit of which Professor Gayley
has admirably caught in English[4]:

> By God, I swear to you
> Unless you "cough up" true,
> You thief, I'll beat you blue,
>   I will, no fear!
> So hand me back my stuff that I put here!

The amount of whipping and other stage "business" to accompany this recitative might safely be trusted to choir boy impromptu. The Latin text of the play at this point gives the following simple directions: "Then St. Nicholas shall go to the thieves and say to them:"

In four Latin stanzas he tells the thieves that he has been whipped because he cannot restore the things left in his charge, and threatens:

> " Quod si non feceritis
>   suspensi cras eritis
>   crucis in patibulo;
>   vestra namque turpia,
>   vestra latrocinia,
>   nuntiabo populo."

(If you don't do this, you will be hanged to-morrow on a gibbet, for your misdeeds and thievery, I will proclaim abroad.)

The threats have the desired effect on the thieves, who in fear return the goods, with no accompanying words provided by the playwright.

When Barbarus finds his treasures again, in a

series of three macaronic stanzas, Latin and
French, he expresses his joy and surprise, ending
with praise for the guardian:

> " Quam bona custodia
>   jo en ai;
>   qua redduntur omnia!
>   De si grant mervegle en ai."

(What a good watch I have had! it returns everything. I am quite surprised.)

The alternating lines in French form a refrain
in which, as in the other songs, the other choir
boys have a chance to join.

Then Barbarus approaches the image and in
three like stanzas, Latin and French, expresses
his gratitude.

At this point St. Nicholas in person makes his
appearance. He disclaims any credit to himself,
and bids Barbarus praise God alone, through
Whom his things have been restored.

Barbarus in reply renounces heathen faith and
praises God, the maker of heaven and earth and
sea, Who has forgiven his sin.

The printed text of the little play is simple
enough, but the easy swing of the series of Latin
songs and the French refrains offering opportunity for choral participation, the beating of the

image, and the impromptu comedy "business" which choir boys might be counted on to supply, would provide as much entertainment at a church festival to-day as they doubtless did in the St. Nicholas' eve celebration of the twelfth century.

In a single manuscript there are preserved four St. Nicholas plays of a century later. The stories presented in these plays are the four mentioned above. The play of the abducted son of Getro may here represent the series.

This Latin play, [5] almost entirely in rimed couplets, is more serious in tone and in general a more elaborate production than the little play by Hilarius. It was staged in characteristic medieval fashion, with simultaneous set; that is to say, there were a number of prepared stations, side by side, all visible, and the action shifted from one station to another. A rubric in the manuscript indicates the stage arrangement.

In order to represent how St. Nicholas freed the son of Getro from the hands of Marmorinus, King of the Agarenes, King Marmorinus shall appear, surrounded by armed servitors and seated on a high seat as if in his own kingdom. In another place, shall be represented Excoranda, the city of Getro, and in it Getro, with his consolers, his wife Euphrosina and their son Adeodatus. East of the city of Excor-

anda shall be the church of St. Nicholas in which
the boy is taken captive.

The action shifts from one of these stations to the
other, all the stations and all the characters, however, being constantly visible.

In the opening scene the servitors approach
King Marmorinus, and, "either all together, or the
first one speaking for all," say:

Hail prince, hail greatest king. Do not delay to
declare thy will to thy servants; we are ready to do
what thou dost wish.

These words apparently are sung, since they are
in rimed verse and since song alone would be appropriate for speech in unison. The king replies:

Go then, do not delay, and subject to my rule
whatever people you can; kill any that resist.

With this the action shifts to another station.

"In the meantime Getro and Euphrosina with
a band of schoolboys," the stage directions tell
us, "shall go to the church of St. Nicholas, to
celebrate his festival, and shall bring with them
their son; and when they shall see the armed servitors of the king coming there, they shall flee
to their own city, in their fright forgetting the
boy. But the servitors of the king shall seize

the boy and bring him into the presence of the king, and either the second of them or all in unison shall say," apparently in song:

We have done, O king, what thou didst order; we have subjected many people to thee and of the things acquired, we are bringing to thee this boy.

Then the third one, or all in unison, shall say:

The boy is fair of face, of active mind, and noble race; it is fitting, in our opinion, that he enter thy service.

The king:

Praise be to Apollo who rules all, and thanks to you who have made so many countries subject and tributary.

And then, addressing the boy:

Good boy, tell us, what is thy land, what thy race; what is the faith of the people of thy country; are they gentile or Christian?

The boy:

My father, Getro by name, is prince of the people of Excoranda; he worships God, who rules the seas, who made us and thee and all things.

The king:

My god, Apollo, is the god that made me. He is true and good. He rules the land, he reigns in the air; him alone we ought to believe in.

The boy:

Thy god is false and evil; he is stupid, blind, deaf, and mute. Thou shouldst not worship such a god, who cannot rule even himself.

The king:

Say not such things; do not offend my god; for if thou dost make him angry, thou canst not in any way escape.

In the meantime, the directions tell us, Euphrosina shall discover that her son has been forgotten and shall return to the church. And when she shall not find the boy, she shall sing the following *Miserere:*

> "Heu! heu! heu mihi miseræ!
>   Quid nunc agam? Quid quæm dicere?
>   Quo peccato merui perdere
>   natum meum, et ultra vivere?
>
>   Cur me pater infelix genuit?
>   Cur me mater infelix abluit?
>   Cur me nutrix lactare debuit?
>   Mortem mihi quare non præbuit?"

The consolers shall come to her and say:

In what way does this grieving aid? Cease to weep, and pray for thy son to the highest Father, and he will give him aid.

Euphrosina, not heeding the words of consolation, shall continue:

Dear son, most beloved child; child, the great part of my soul; now thou art to us the cause of sadness who wert the cause of joy.

Comforters:

Do not despair of the grace of God. He whose great mercy gave thee this boy, will return to thee either him or another.

Euphrosina:

My soul is disturbed within me. Why should death delay? When I am not able to see thee, my son, I prefer to die rather than to live.

Comforters:

Struggle, grief, and despair injure thee and do not profit thy son; instead, from thy wealth give to schoolboys and to the poor. Ask the kindness of Nicholas that he may pray for the mercy of the Father on high for thy son, that thy prayer may not fail.

Euphrosina (praying to St. Nicholas):

Nicholas, most holy father, Nicholas most dear to
God, if thou wishest that I should worship thee longer,
cause my son to return. Thou that didst save many
in the sea, and three men from the bonds of death,
listen to the prayer of me, a suppliant, and assure me
that it will be granted. I will not eat of flesh longer,
nor partake of wine, nor enjoy anything more until
my son shall return.

Getro:

Dear sister, cease to mourn: thy tears avail thee
nothing. But seek the propitiation of the Father
on high for our son. To-morrow is the festival of
St. Nicholas whom all Christianity ought to worship,
to venerate, to bless. Hear, then, my counsel. Let
us go to his festival. Let us praise his greatness and
seek his support. Perhaps it is an inspiration of
God that admonishes me on account of our son. With
the grace of God we must pray for the great kindness
of Nicholas.

Then they shall get up and go to the church
of St. Nicholas. And when they have entered,
Euphrosina shall stretch her hands out toward
heaven and say:

Highest Father, king of all kings, sole king, and sole
hope of mortals, make to be returned to us our son,
the solace of our life. Hear the prayers of us suppli-

ant.   Thou that didst send thy Son into the world
to make us citizens of Heaven, to save us from the
bars of hell.   Father God, thou whose power dost
supply everything good, do not cast off me a sinner,
but let me see again my son.   Nicholas, whom we
call a saint, if all is true that we believe concerning
thee, let thy prayers go forth to God for us and our
son.

"After these words," the directions tell us, "she
shall leave the church and go home and there
prepare a table with bread and wine for the entertainment of schoolboys and the poor.   When
these have been invited and have begun to eat,
Marmorinus (at the other end of the stage) shall
say to his servitors":

My beloved, I want to tell you that I have never
in my life felt such hunger as I have to-day.   I can't
stand it.   Make ready what I ought to eat and save
my life.   Why delay?   Go quickly, prepare at once
something for me to eat.

The servitors then shall go and bear food to
the king and shall say:

We have prepared the food as thou didst command
and here it is.   Now if thou dost wish, thou mayst
grow fat in extinguishing thy hunger.

Then water is brought, and the king washes his
hands and begins to eat and says:

I was hungry, now I am thirsty. Bring me wine, and no delay about it, my servant, son of Getro.

The boy, hearing this, shall sigh deeply, saying to himself:

Alas! Alas, poor me! I should like to die, for as long as I live, I shall never be free.

The king, addressing the boy:

Why dost thou sigh so? What ails thee? What dost thou want?

The boy:

I was thinking of my misery, of my father and my native land. I began to sigh, and said to myself, "It is a year to-day since I entered this country, and was made a miserable slave, subject to royal power."

The king:

Poor wretch, why dost thou think about it? What good does thy grieving do? None can take thee from me as long as I do not care to lose thee.

"In the meantime," the directions tell us, "some one in the likeness of Nicholas shall take up the boy holding in his hand the cup with fresh wine, and shall place him before his father's city and, as if not seen, shall depart. Then one of the citizens shall say to the boy":

Boy, who art thou, and where goest thou? Who gave thee the cup with the fresh wine?

The boy:

I am here and am not going farther. I am the only son of Getro. Glory and praise to Nicholas whose grace brought me back here.

Then that citizen shall run to Getro and say:

Be glad, Getro. Weep no more. Outside stands thy son. Praise be to Nicholas whose grace restored him.

"When Euphrosina hears this message, she shall run, and after kissing and embracing her son many times, shall say":

To our God be glory and praise. Whose great mercy, turning our grief to joy, has released our son. To our father Nicholas be enduring praise and thanks, whose prayer to God aided us in this affair.

The play ends with the choral singing of the Latin hymn to St. Nicholas, beginning with the words "*Copiosæ Caritatis.*"

As already remarked, these Latin plays of St.

Nicholas are the earliest plays handling subjects outside the scriptural narrative, also one of the St. Nicholas stories is the subject of one of the group of plays by the earliest medieval dramatist known by name. In another way the name of St. Nicholas is associated with the beginnings of the modern drama, in that one of the St. Nicholas stories provides the theme for one of the earliest of plays in a vernacular tongue and produced under secular control. The play in question is the famous one by Jean Bodel produced at Arras in the very first years of the thirteenth century. The time of production was probably the eve of St. Nicholas' day, and the producing actors were the members of a secular fraternity of which St. Nicholas was the patron saint, possibly, Gaston Paris[6] suggests, the famous minstrel brotherhood at Arras that had for its palladium the famous candle, said to have set itself on the viol of one of the brotherhood while he played before the altar.

The story told in this play is one already well known as a subject for dramatic rendering in Latin, one of three handled by Hilarius, the story of the image of St. Nicholas and the robbers. But in this vernacular play St. Nicholas himself is overshadowed by the new elements that have been joined to the story. The Jew, or pagan, of earlier versions of the story, here appears as a Saracen king at war with the Christians. The thieves are tavern revelers who steal in order to pay their tavern score.

In condensed summary, following largely the summary by Creizenach,[7] the story runs as follows:

After a prolog in which the content of the story is related, the messenger Auberon appears and announces to the king that the Christians have invaded his land. The king is enraged at his idol Tervagant that this has been possible in spite of the fact that the image has recently been richly gilded. Auberon is sent forth to summon the emirs with their armies. There follows a scene between the Christians and Saracens, which is imbued with all the ardor and spirit of the crusading times. The Christians show divinely inspired bravery and are visited by an angel which encourages them in the fight. They are defeated in battle, but the angel announces that they have won a place in Paradise. The Saracens find on the battlefield only one Christian alive, and he is kneeling before an image of St. Nicholas. The man with his image is brought before the Saracen king, who in ridicule asks what the ugly old chap

is good for. The Christian announces that the
image is excellent as a protector of treasure. The
king determines to test the image and causes his
herald Connart to proclaim that the treasure will
be left open, guarded only by the image of St.
Nicholas. The Christian prisoner is given over
to the hangman Durand to die if his patron saint
does not live up to his reputation.

The scene shifts to a tavern. The innkeeper
has his man servant announce that he has a fine
wine for the epicure, a wine which he describes in
most eloquent fashion. The rogues assemble,
and in a drawn-out scene manifest their appreciation of the good wine, but at the end are unable to
pay their score. They determine to steal the
unguarded royal treasure, and the innkeeper
agrees to receive the stolen goods. They enter
the treasure chamber, and with great labor, which
affords much comedy, get away with the heavy
chest.

The theft is discovered, and the Christian prisoner is ordered to be hanged, but gets a suspended
sentence of one day, and cheered by an angel,
awaits the intervention of the saint.

The thieves, in the meantime, have brought
the treasure to the tavern and continue their
revelry until they fall asleep. Hardly has sleep

overtaken them, when the saint appears and in
gruff language demands the return of the treasure,
with the gallows as the alternative.　The thieves,
panic-stricken, carry the treasure back.　One of
them proposes that each take a handful of gold
pieces, but they are too much terrified, and in the
end the ringleader must leave his mantle with the
innkeeper in settlement.

The king, delighted at the protection afforded,
takes the Christian into high favor, naturally to
the disappointment of the hangman.　He also
decides to abjure his old faith, and his emirs feel
it their feudal duty to follow his example, with the
exception of one, who, however, is compelled to
kneel before the saint's image.　In the midst of
all this the image of Tervagant utters a frightful
shriek, but is, by command of the king, cast out
of the "Synagogue" in shame and disgrace while
the Christian starts a *Te Deum*, in which the actors,
and, perhaps, the spectators, join.

In this play it will be observed that the old
story is made to serve a new purpose.　St. Nicholas
is made an exponent of the virtue of Christianity
as opposed to the Saracen faith.　The story is
developed with much supporting detail.　The
struggle between Christian and Saracen is represented with true crusading zeal, in the spirit

which pervaded the contemporary romances of
Charlemagne and his paladins. On the other
hand, balancing with these scenes, noble in tone,
were the low comedy scenes provided by the tavern
revelers, drinking, casting dice, quarreling, and
speaking a slang often unintelligible to the modern
reader, in general affording remarkable genre
pictures of French life in the early thirteenth
century.

In his two-sided development of the dramatic
values in this story, the author established a
method which one might have expected to be followed by his contemporaries, a method actually
followed, a little later, in the development of the
native English drama. In reality, however, the
play occupies a solitary position in its own day and
age. To the author must be given the credit of
original creation, of being ahead of his time. But
this credit the author must share with the story of
his play, for has not the name of St. Nicholas
through all the centuries, down to our own time,
been constantly associated, not only with the
idea of noble beneficence, but with a peculiar
quality of good nature and fun?

CHAPTER VIII

ST. NICHOLAS AS PATRON SAINT

A NYONE brought up in a Protestant country, in the Protestant faith, will not find it easy to form an adequate conception of the nature of saint worship. Such a person, however, if he should visit certain of the less progressive provinces of Catholic Christendom, would find surviving in much of its pristine vigor, with much of its original *naïveté*, the saint worship once universal in the Christian world. In Sicily, for instance, he would find each city with its patron saint revered and honored very much as in the earlier days. If he should happen to be in Catania on one of the two days in the year devoted to the honor of Catania's patron saint Agatha, he would see the image of St. Agatha surrounded by native offerings of extravagant value, in a resplendent car drawn by white-robed men, and he would hear enthusiastic shouts of "Viva Sant' Agatha!" whenever a new candle for the car was offered by

Triumphal Car of St. Lucy used in the Annual Procession in Honor
of the Saint at Syracuse in Sicily.

one of the votaries of the saint.   In Palermo he
would find like honor paid on her festival day to
St. Rosalia, the patron saint of Palermo; in Syracuse he would find St. Lucy; in Taormina, St.
Pancras, similarly honored.   These Sicilian celebrations of saints' days, featured as they are by
the presence of such modern, ultra-secular inven-
tions as fireworks, nevertheless retain not only
much of the form but to some extent the spirit
of earlier celebrations.

Nor is the Sicilian worship of saints entirely
one-sided.   On the one hand honors are paid, but
on the other hand benefits are supposed to be received.   An idea of the nature of the protection
afforded by the saints and of the intimate relation
existing between saint and votary may be gained
by a visit to the church of San Nicola at Girgenti.
There one will find the picture of the saint surrounded by representations, in silver, or more
often in wax or carved and painted wood, of swollen
limb, cancerous breast, goitered throat, injured
eye, carbuncle, and the like, healed through the
intervention of the saint.   Even more specific,
more living, record of protection received is afforded by the votive offerings on one wall of the
church in the form of naïve little paintings illus-
trating the aid afforded by St. Nicholas, one

8

"showing a spirited donkey running away with a painted cart, the terrified occupant frantically making signals of distress to S. Nicola in heaven who is preparing promptly to check the raging ass, others showing S. Nicola drawing a petitioner from the sea, or turning a mafia dagger aside, or finding a lost child in the mountains."[1]

In Catholic Brittany, too, one will find similar forms of saint worship.   One will find the so-called "Pardons," or pilgrimages on different days of the year to different ones of the famous shrines of Brittany, occasions celebrated with festal processions accompanying the image or the relics of the saint honored.   In the Breton churches also one will find the same form of testimony, as in Sicily, to the protection offered by the various saints.   In the church of St. Sauveur at Dinan, in the chapel of St. Roch, one will find a representation of the saint over the altar and on the wall a framed *vœu*, to the effect that St. Roch confers many benefits, especially in case of pestilence, that he saved the city from pestilence in 16—, and that the *vœu* is for the sake of preserving the memory of his goodness to the city.   On the wall also are framed litanies to St. Roch and individual votive offerings with dates, many in the form of hearts, others framed inscriptions with "*Merci Bon*

St. Roch," accompanied by the date of the benefit received.   Over the door of a house in Brittany also one often finds the image of the patron saint of the occupant.

In Brittany down to our own time honor continues to be paid to a great number of saints not known elsewhere, never canonized by the Roman church and probably in their origin having little of Christian character, more than likely Christian representatives of earlier, local, pagan divinities. The functions of these local Breton saints are specialized to an extent hardly found elsewhere at the present time.   Ailments are subject to the cure of particular saints.   The specialization is hardly equalled even by that in the modern practice of medicine.   Saint Mamert is invoked in case of pains of the stomach, Saint Méen for insanity, Saint Hubert for dog bites, Saint Livertin for headache, Saint Houarniaule for fear, Saint Radegonde for toothache.

There is a certain beauty in the intimate relations existing between simple people and their divine representative, but the naïve character of the practice, in a striking manner, brings to one's realization the superstitious mode of thought prevalent in medieval times.   The Reformation, in the sixteenth century, did much to dispel these older, superstitious forms of religious thought. As already remarked, among Protestants the old reverence of the saints is hardly understood. In the modern Catholic church, too, the extravagant features of saintly legend and of saint worship have been largely eliminated, only vestiges surviving in those provinces little affected by modern progress.

Evidence of similar specialization in earlier forms of saint worship, and of Protestant ridicule of it, is to be found in Barnabe Googe's sixteenth-century translations from Naogeorgus[2]:

To every saint they also doe his office here assine,
And fourtene doe they count of whom thou mayst
    have ayde divine;

. . . .

Saint Barbara lookes that none without the body of
    Christ doe dye,
Saint Cathern favours learned men, and gives them
    wisdome hye;

. . . .

Saint Appolin the rotten teeth doth helpe, when sore
    they ake;
Otilla from the bleared eyes the cause and griefe doth
    take;

. . . .

Saint Gertrude riddes the house of mise, and killeth
    all the rattes;
The like doth bishop Huldrich with his earth, two
    passing cattes;

Images of Breton Saints, Preserved at Moncontour-de-Bretagne.

Saint Gregerie lookes to little boys, to teach their
    a, b, c,
And makes them for to love their bookes and schollers
    good to be;
Saint Nicolas keepes the mariners from daunger
    and diseas
That beaten are with boystrous waves and tost in
    dreadfull seas.

Not only were the saints invoked for protection
against particular ills, but the guilds, or craft
fraternities, had each its patron saint. Cities
and nations also had each its particular saintly
guardian, and individuals, by assuming the names
of particular saints, aimed to establish a protective
relationship. Variations in these relationships
existed, but some ones widely recognized were
that between St. Agatha and nurses, St. Catherine
and St. Gregory and studious persons, St. Cecilia
and musicians, Saints Cosmas and Damian and
physicians, St. Luke and painters, St. Sebastian
and archers, St. Valentine and lovers, St. Ives and
lawyers, Saints Andrew and Joseph and carpen-
ters, St. George and clothiers, and so on. Of
countries Scotland comes under the care of St.
Andrew, England under that of St. George, Ire-
land under that of St. Patrick, Wales under that
of St. David. St. Anthony belongs especially to
Italy, St. Denis to France, St. Thomas to Spain,

St. Mary to Holland, St. Sebastian to Portugal. Of cities Venice is under the protection of St. Mark, Florence of St. John, Paris of St. Genevieve, Vienna of St. Stephen, Cologne of the Holy Magi.[3]

As compared with some of the other saints in affording protection St. Nicholas is less the specialist and more the general practitioner. He certainly has his share of duties assigned him. With St. Mary and St. Andrew he shares the guardianship of Russia, with Olaf that of Norway,[4] with St. Julian of Rimini, that of the whole eastern coast of Italy. Of cities he is the patron saint: in the North, of Moscow and Aberdeen, in the South, of Bari and Corfu, in intermediate countries, of Amiens, Civray (Poitou), Ancona, Fribourg (Switzerland), and several places in Lorraine.[5]

The guardianship of St. Nicholas over schoolboys and unwedded maids has already been discussed. Mention has also been made of St. Nicholas as patron saint of various crafts in the towns of the Netherlands. To the list of occupations protected, may be added those of butchers, fishermen, pilgrims, brewers, chandlers, and coopers,[6] with all of which St. Nicholas is more or less closely associated as patron saint. It remains to consider in more detail the part played by St.

Anderson

Beato Angelico.   St. Nicholas Saves the City in Time of Famine.

Nicholas as the protector of mariners and the less prominent, but not the less interesting, relationship between St. Nicholas and thieves.

Throughout the Christian world, everywhere, the devotion of sailors to St. Nicholas is much in evidence. In Greece, where St. Nicholas is one of the most popularly honored saints, at the present day, according to a recent authority,[7] "everyone connected with seafaring appeals to him for protection and relief. All ships and boats carry his ikon with an ever-burning lamp, and in his chapels, models of boats, coils of cables, anchors, and such things, are given as votive offerings. Pirates even used to give him half their booty in gratitude for favors received. On account of this worship, St. Nicholas has been said to have supplanted Poseidon, for the cults lie along the same lines. During a recent strike at the Piræus the seamen swore by St. Nicholas not to yield, and they would not break their vow although they wished to compromise. The Archbishop had to come specially to release them from their oath."

In Russia, as in Greece, an ikon of St. Nicholas is carried in every merchantman.[8] In other countries there is plentiful record of similar association of St. Nicholas with the protection of the sea. In the Island of Minorca, in the eighteenth

century, near the entrance to the harbor, stood a
chapel dedicated to St. Nicholas, to which, according to an old account, "the sailors resort that have
suffered shipwreck, to return thanks for their
preservation, and to hang up votive pictures
(representing the dangers they have escaped),
in gratitude to the saint for the protection he
vouchsafed them, and in accomplishment of the
vows they made in the height of the storm."[9]

In Teutonic countries St. Nicholas played a
similar part. In Germany it was formerly customary for sailors escaped from shipwreck to dedi-
cate a piece of old sail to St. Nicholas.[10] In every
Hanseatic city there was a church to St. Nicholas,
and in Hanseatic cities favorite personal names
were Nicolaus, Claas, Nickelo, and other popular
derivatives from St. Nicholas. There were also
churches dedicated to St. Nicholas in places
threatened by injury from water, for instance at
Quedlingburg. In Switzerland, too, St. Nicholas
is the patron of travelers by water. Sailors on the
Lake of Lucerne are said to make vows and votive
offerings to him, and by Swiss waters formerly
there were everywhere to be found St. Nicholas
chapels.[11]

The association of St. Nicholas with the sea is
found in one of the best known of the incidents in

his legend, although, in this case, even more than the case of the other incidents of his life story, there is room for question whether he is to be regarded as the protector of seamen because of the incident in his story, or the incident in the story originated as an explanation of the veneration paid St. Nicholas by seamen.

The incident in question is thus recorded in the Golden Legend:

It is read in a chronicle that the blessed Nicholas was at the Council of Nice; and on a day as a ship with mariners were in perishing on the sea, they prayed and required devoutly Nicholas, servant of God, saying: If those things that we have heard of thee be true, prove them now.   And anon a man appeared in his likeness and said: Lo! see ye me not? ye called me, and then he began to help them in their exploit of the sea, and anon the tempest ceased.   And when they were come to his church, they knew him without any man to show him to them, and yet they had never seen him.   And then they thanked God and him of their deliverance.   And he bade them to attribute it to the mercy of God, and to their belief, and nothing to his merits.

It is worthy of note that the mariners of this story, when in distress, already know of the reputation of St. Nicholas for efficacy in such situations, which seems to indicate that in this case story grew from belief rather than belief from story.

The story of the rescue at sea accomplished by the intervention of the saint forms a favorite subject for Italian painters, particularly those of the earlier period. The picture by L. Monaco represents the scene in a manner delightfully primitive.

The aid afforded by St. Nicholas to mariners in distress also forms the subject of a story sung in a popular Servian carol,[12] in which there is much in evidence the peculiar charm of the folk-tale. The story goes that all the saints, festively assembled, were drinking wine. When the cup, out of which each drank in turn, was passed to St. Nicholas, he was too sleepy to hold it, and let it drop. St. Elias shook him by the arm and aroused him. "Oh! I beg the pardon of the company," said the sleepy saint, "but I have been very busy and I was absent from your festival. The sea was rough, and I had to give my help to three hundred ships that were in danger."

It is not easy to associate St. Nicholas with the thought of severity. One can hardly conceive of him as a stern judge. Was he open to the charge of being what is popularly called "easy"? Certain it is that his beneficence had a wide scope. The universality of his guardianship can hardly be better illustrated than by the fact that he not only

L. Monaco.   St. Nicholas Rescues the Seamen.

afforded protection from robbers and shielded the
unjustly condemned, but at the same time shared
with St. Dismas the questionable honor of being
the protector of pirates and thieves.

This protective relationship, in Elizabethan
times, formed the subject of a stock jest. Robbers
and thieves were facetiously called "St. Nicholas'
clerks."

"Sirrah," says Gadshill, "if they meet not with
St. Nicholas' clerks, I'll give thee this neck."

"No," rejoins the Chamberlain, "I'll none of
it; I pr'ythee keep that for the hangman; for I
know thou worshipp'st Saint Nicholas as truly
as a man of falsehood may."[13]

How did St. Nicholas get into such evil associations? It will be remembered that the seamen
protected by him included pirates, and that Greek
pirates are said to have shared their booty with
him. Have these evil associations corrupted his
good manners, and has he thus been brought into
association with thieves and robbers? Perhaps
so. But other explanations have been offered.
His name has become associated with that of
the "Old Nick" in a way that remains to be explained. Perhaps in this way he has come to
acquire the function of the "Old Nick," as the
protector of evil. A more plausible explanation

accounts for his association with thieves by the
popularly known story, which formed the subject
of one of the St. Nicholas plays, that of the thieves
who had stolen goods left under the guardianship
of St. Nicholas' image and who were compelled
by the saint to restore the goods and thus brought
"to the way of trouth."

Whatever the cause, the association was one
well established. St. Nicholas' clerks were well
known in Elizabethan times,[14] and are frequently referred to in literature. There were also
lively popular stories on the subject, one of which
forms the subject of a stanza in a merry St. Nicholas carol.[15]

> "Another he dede sekyrly,
> He saved a thief that was ful sly,
> That stal a swyn out of his sty,
> His lyf than savyd he."

CHAPTER IX

PAGAN HERITAGE OF ST. NICHOLAS

IT is well known that when paganism was superseded by Christianity, the older religion was by no means obliterated. In Greece the pagan temples often were converted into Christian churches. At Athens, the Parthenon, a temple of the Virgin Pallas, became a church of the Virgin Mary; the temple of Theseus became a church devoted to a Christian hero, also a dragon-slayer, St. George of Cappadocia. In the structure of new churches, material from the older temples was freely used. In many of the churches of Rome may be seen beautiful classical columns taken from the earlier pagan structures. A fine instance of the mingling of elements, old and new, in Christian architecture, is to be seen at Syracuse in Sicily, where the older classical temple of Minerva has been transformed into a renaissance cathedral. The columns of the Doric temple are built into the wall of the church but are too thick to be concealed. On the outside they may be seen, at times a protruding Doric capital, at times a whole Doric column; within the church, they form a line of magnificent weathered columns bordering the outer side of each aisle. In this church, to the Christian and pagan combination, is superadded a third element, in the form of rounded Saracenic battlements.

The hybrid nature of this Christian architecture in the countries pervaded by classical civilization finds a striking parallel in the Christian practices and Christian beliefs of these countries. In these, too, there is evident a mingling of elements new and old, Christian and pagan, with here and there a tinge taken on from later forms of non-Christian religion, corresponding to the Saracenic element in the architecture of the cathedral at Syracuse. Just as the graceful classic columns survive as beautiful features in the Christian churches, so, many fair products of the poetic imagination belonging to the earlier faith have found a place in the Christian religion. This is particularly true in the case of the saints, who continue to exert over the forces of nature the same control in the interests of man that the minor gods and demi-gods had done before.

In modern Greece there is to be found ample

illustration of Christian appropriation of the old. When gods have not been directly transformed into saints, at least many of their attributes have been taken over. In the island of Naxos, St. Dionysios is widely worshiped, and like the god of similar name, is connected in popular story with the origin of the wine. There is a story of the journey of the saint from Mt. Olympos to Naxos, in which there is assuredly more of the pagan than of the saintly quality. "He [St. Dionysios] noticed an herb by the way and planted it in the bone of a bird, then in the bone of a lion, and lastly in the bone of an ass. At Naxos he made the first wine with its fruit. The intoxication which followed the drinking of this wine had three stages: first, he sang like a bird; then, felt strong as a lion; and lastly, became foolish as an ass." [1] In a similar way, St. Demetrios, as the popular patron of Greek husbandmen and shepherds, and the protector of agriculture in general, assumes the functions of the Earth-Mother, Demeter, [2] and St. Artemidos, as patron of weakly children, has taken over some of the attributes of Artemis, to whom belonged protecting powers over children, animals, and vegetation. [3] Still better known is the case of St. Elias, who has acquired many of the attributes of the sun-god, Helios. "It would be difficult to find any spot in Greece from which one could not descry on a prominent hilltop a little white chapel dedicated to him, where at least once a year, on the 20th of July, a service is held. This hilltop saint is believed by the peasants to be lord of sunshine, rain, and thunder."[4]

Venus, too, finds her place in Christian worship under the name of St. Venere. In West Albania, where the practice has been imported from the south of Italy, "she is invoked by girls as patroness of marriage."[5] In the territory of St. Sophia, in Calabria, her festival is celebrated on the 27th of July, and the girls sing a song, in substance "a prayer to St. Venere not to leave them husbandless now that all their companions are married and gone."[6] St. Merkurios, also, has many of the attributes of the pagan god Mercury. There is an ancient story in which the saint plays the rôle of messenger formerly assigned to the god. Basil, Bishop of Cæsarea, in a vision, saw the heavens open, revealing Christ enthroned. "Then Christ called, 'Merkurios, go and slay Julian the King, the persecutor of the Christians.' And St. Merkurios stood before Him wearing a gleaming iron breastplate, and on hearing the command, he disappeared. Then he reappeared and stood before the Lord and cried, 'Julian the King has been slain as Thou didst command, O Lord.'"[7]

In many other cases, where the direct pagan inheritance is not so easily traced, saints in modern Greece accomplish functions precisely similar to those accomplished in ancient times by minor deities. St. George is regarded as the protector of the crops, probably on account of the etymology of his name (*Ge* = "earth," *ergein* = "work"). For a similar reason, apparently, St. Maura is invoked in case of ulcers or smallpox. Other saints with similar functions are St. Madertos invoked in case of pestilence among beasts, St. Blasios in case of sore throat, and St. John in cases of fever.

People accustomed to seek divine aid in this way, in case of trouble, are not easily to be deprived of their recourse. If they are forbidden to worship their pagan divinities, then substitutes must be found. Thus seamen deprived of Poseidon as source of aid, had recourse to St. Phokas and later turned to St. Nicholas, possibly, as has been pointed out, due to the story, in the legend of St. Nicholas, of aid rendered by him to the ship in distress. The connection once established, St. Nicholas came more and more to occupy the place formerly held by Poseidon. Hence probably the position held by St. Nicholas in popular be-

9

lief, especially in eastern Christendom, as the guardian of sailors.

There is one modern Greek story of St. Nicholas as patron saint of seamen which deserves to be told because it shows the occasional survival, in the popular worship of saints, of pagan elements which the Christian Church could not countenance. The story, as told by an old Greek man, is to this effect: "At the time of the Revolution a number of Greek ships assembled off Kamári. There was great excitement and trepidation. So they thought things over and decided to send a man to St. Nicholas to ask him that their ships might prosper in the war. They accordingly seized a man and took him to the large hall at Kamári. There they cut off his head and his hands, and carried him down the steps into the hall." This was a pagan rite obviously not to be tolerated by the Christian God, for the story goes, "thereupon God appeared with a bright torch in his hand, and the bearers of the body dropped it, and all present fled in terror."[8]

It is evident that St. Nicholas inherited some of the attributes of Poseidon, or Neptune. But that does not sum up the extent of his pagan heritage. Probably earlier than the association of St. Nicholas with Poseidon is that with Demeter, or Diana, whose cult was particularly in vogue in Lycia, the scene of the principal events in the story of St. Nicholas.

In the Eastern Church there were two celebrations in honor of St. Nicholas, not only the one on the 6th of December, but one on the 9th of May. The May celebration, which is still kept up by Italians, even in America, is usually said to be in honor of the removal of the relics of St. Nicholas to Bari, but not unlikely is the continuation of the Rosalia, a local pagan spring festival at Myra, the Lycian home of St. Nicholas. Not only in Lycia, but elsewhere, the St. Nicholas cult supplanted the earlier worship of Artemis. In Ætolia "at the village of Kephalovryso, there is a little ruined temple of St. Nicholas which, according to an inscription built into the church, stands on the site of a temple of Artemis. Another instance of the same transference occurs at Aulis, where a little Byzantine church of St. Nicholas has replaced the Artemisium."[9]

Following the substitution of the Christian worship of St. Nicholas for the pagan worship of Artemis, there were two natural consequences. In the first place the pagan deity, formerly revered, came to be regarded as an evil spirit. In the second place this evil spirit was supposed to be particularly hostile to the Christian saint that had replaced her in popular worship. This hostility is reflected in the well-known story of the devil's plot against the church of St. Nicholas. The Golden Legend version of the story is as follows:

And in this country the people served idols and worshiped the false image of the cursed Diana. And to the time of this holy man, many of them had some customs of the paynims, for to sacrifice to Diana under a sacred tree; but this good man made them of all the country to cease then these customs, and commanded to cut off the tree. Then the devil was angry and wroth against him and made an oil that burned, against nature, in water, and burned stones also. And then he transformed him in the guise of a religious woman, and put him in a little boat, and encountered pilgrims that sailed in the sea towards this holy saint, and areasoned them thus, and said: I would fain go to this holy man, but I may not, wherefore I pray you to bear this oil into his church, and for the remembrance of me, that ye anoint the walls of the hall; and anon he vanished away. Then they saw anon after another ship with honest persons, among whom there was one like to S. Nicholas, which spake to them softly: What hath this woman said to you, and what hath she brought? And they told to him all by order. And he said to them: This is the evil and foul Diana; and to the end that ye know that I say truth, cast that oil into the sea. And when they had cast it, a great fire caught it in the sea, and they saw it long burn against nature. Then they came to this holy man and said to him: Verily thou art he that appeared to us in the sea and deliveredst us from the sea and awaits of the devil.

But the victory over the pagan deity was not a complete one. Constant association of St. Nicholas custom with earlier worship of Artemis was not without its influence on the popular conception of the Christian saint. One is tempted to assume the malevolent and insidious work of the pagan deity aiming to corrupt the character of the benevolent bishop. In any event from Artemis as well as from Poseidon St. Nicholas inherited attributes which serve to explain some of the elements in his complex personality. It is to be remembered that Artemis of Ephesus was not only a spring deity but also in part a sea and a river goddess. Hence her epithet, "Potamia." Both associations, that with spring, and especially that with the sea, Artemis shares with St. Nicholas.[10] Artemis-Cybele is often represented as a sea monster with the tail of a fish. There are traces of a similar grotesque popular conception of St. Nicholas in the Sicilian popular legend with the hero named Nicolo-Pesce. This conception of St. Nicholas is much in evidence in western Europe and serves to explain the connection of St. Nicholas with a conception widely prevalent there, of a water spirit or god. Among Teutonic peoples, particularly, this water spirit is widely known with various names, such as Nix, Nickel, Nickelman, Nick, Nökke. Millers are said to be particularly afraid of this spirit and to throw different things into the water on the sixth day of December, St. Nicholas' day, to propitiate it.[11] In the character of Nikur, a Protean water sprite (Edda, *Doemesaga*, 3), he inhabits the lakes and rivers of Scandinavia, where he raises sudden storms and tempests and leads mankind into destruction.[12] Danish peasantry, in earlier times, conceived of the Nökke (Nikke) as a monster with human head, dwelling both in fresh and in salt water. Where anyone was drowned, they said, *Nökken tag ham bort*, "the Nökke took him away." The Icelandic Neck, a kelpie or water spirit, appears in the form of a fine horse on the seashore. If anyone is foolish enough to mount him, he gallops off and plunges into the water with his burden.[13]

In France there is known a similar water monster, and there, paradoxical as it may seem, it has taken the name of the benevolent St. Nicholas. It is a terrible monster that seizes fishermen who walk without permission by the water side at nightfall. It has claws and tears the faces of the children that remain too late on the beach.[14]

The water monster under discussion was known in England. Back in the eighth century, in the story of Beowulf, there are introduced water monsters, apparently conceived of as like walruses or sea-lions, but malevolent in character. These are called *niceras*. The "Old Nick," a name familiar since the early seventeenth century, seems to have originated in the conception of this water monster once prevalent in the North of England. The conversion of the name of the water demon into a name for the Devil is not an unusual phenomenon. The process is illustrated in the history of the Greek word "demon" itself, which, at first meaning "spirit," in no evil sense, with the hostile attitude assumed toward earlier religious conceptions following the introduction of Christianity, came to be used as a name for an evil spirit or devil. The same conversion of an old name to a new use is to be seen in the case of the "Old Nick," in the beginning the name of a water spirit, later a name for the Devil. In this case the malevolent character of the water spirit made the conversion one easy to comprehend.

What, then, is the relation of this well known, usually malevolent, water spirit to St. Nicholas?

An attempt has recently been made to show that the Eastern conception of St. Nicholas as a water spirit, originating in the older mythical beliefs concerning Artemis, was carried by seamen to the West of Europe and that in this way the name St. Nicholas is the base of the different forms for the name of the water spirit.[15] This theory can hardly be sustained, since there is no proof of the popularity of St. Nicholas in the West so early as the earliest reference to the water spirit, that is to say, in the case of the *niceras* of the English *Beowulf*, and because in popular contraction of the name Nicholas, it is the second part of the name, the -clas, that usually survives. A more likely explanation is that the confusion between the water spirit, variously known as Nick, Neck, Nicor, Nökke, Nickel, Nickelmann, and St. Nicholas, is explained by a well-known process of popular etymology. St. Nicholas with his attributes as controller of the waters, inherited from the mythical Poseidon and Artemis, when in the eleventh century he became known in the West, became confused with the more and more vaguely conceived pagan water spirit of similar name, and in the end, in certain places, became identified with him, thereby inheriting some of his qualities, and influencing the form of his name.

Over in Russia also St. Nicholas has fallen heir to similar attributes.   In this way he has come to figure in an interesting episode in recent musical history, an episode which illustrates in a most interesting way how the influence of St. Nicholas has penetrated to affairs of our own time.   Rimsky-Korsakoff, in his opera, *Sadko*, composed in 1896, made use of an old Novgorod folk-tale of the Volga.   This story centers about a river deity said to be something like the Old Man of the Sea in the Arabian Nights Tales.   Under Christian influence this tale has been converted into a story of St. Nicholas, one of many told of him in Russia, where he is one of the most popular of the saints. Both versions of the popular story persist, the earlier, pagan form and the one where St. Nicholas has inherited the prominent part.   Rimsky-Korsakoff, after some hesitation which of the two versions to use, finally made choice of the later, St. Nicholas, version.   But here he came into conflict with Russian orthodox bureaucracy, which would not permit such irreverent use to be made of the Russian patron saint Nicholas.   The composer, therefore, made a change, substituting the names of the older version.   But in his opera he had made free use of musical themes derived from the liturgy of the St. Nicholas festival, and this music he retained, making a humorous incongruity between the sacred music and the pagan story. A quarrel with officialdom resulted, which is said to have been one of the reasons why Rimsky-Korsakoff lost his position as Director of the Conservatoire at Petrograd.

Attempt has been made to connect St. Nicholas, through his relationship to the Teutonic water spirit, with Odin, who in one of the Edda poems is given the name Hnikar. This particular link between St. Nicholas and Odin has not been successfully established. It is certain, however, that a relationship exists. The time of the St. Nicholas festival, December 6th, and of Christmas, where St. Nicholas has come to play an important part, coincides in part with the season of the year when Odin, as god of the air, made his nightly rides, or, as god of the dead led through the air the troops of spirits of departed ones. The coincidence in time, under Christian influence, led to the transfer to St. Nicholas of some of the functions of Odin. The heritage of St. Nicholas from Odin has been discussed in an earlier chapter. From Odin St. Nicholas inherited his gray horse, which in some Germanic countries he uses in his nightly rides, but which he traded for a reindeer before coming to America. For this horse of St. Nicholas

children in parts of Europe leave the hay and
oats once left for the horse of Odin. From Odin,
too, Santa Claus inherited certain details of his
appearance, most notably his long white beard
as distinguished from the kind of beard familiar
in pictures of the bishop-saint.

From others of the Teutonic gods St. Nicholas
received legacies. In him various scholars[16]
have recognized attributes of Fro and of Niordhr,
the father of Fro. The task of purveying gifts
for children, for which St. Nicholas uses the horse
of Odin, is a function sometimes attributed to the
spirits of the dead, who, with or without Odin as a
leader, in the time of the shortest days of the year
are supposed to revisit their earthly homes.[17]

From this discussion one will see that the
Christian saint Nicholas has the same perplexing
variety of aspects that make it so difficult to form
any single unified conception in the case of one
of the pagan gods. At Bari, in Italy, where his
relics are preserved, on his festival day, he receives
the honors of a water god not necessarily malevolent in character. His image is borne by
sailors in procession out to sea and at nightfall
is escorted back to the cathedral with torches,
fireworks, and chanting.[18] In parts of France
he has inherited different qualities; his name is

given to a water spirit, a veritable ogre in its malevolence. In many other countries, including our own, he has inherited the pleasant rôle of children's benefactor. If one wishes to gain a realization of how popular heroic conceptions are formed, one should compare the many-sided St. Nicholas known in our own day in the various countries of Christendom with the simple figure, as clearly as one may distinguish it, of the kindly youth that was born at Patras in Asia Minor in the early days of Christianity.

CHAPTER X

THROUGHOUT the present discussion of St. Nicholas the fact has been kept constantly prominent that St. Nicholas is more famed for deeds than for doctrine. His rôle was not in general that of the apostle extending the boundaries of Christendom nor that of the expounder of creed. His fame rests on his kindly acts. But it was inevitable that the authority of so beloved and so influential a personage should be invoked in support of orthodoxy. In the Golden Legend mere mention is made of the presence of St. Nicholas at that meeting of critical importance, the Council of Nice. But in the Roman Breviary it is recorded that just before his death he was present at the Council of Nice and there, "with those three hundred and eighteen church fathers, condemned the Arian heresy."

Controversy, particularly religious controversy, has its pitfalls even for those of most gentle nature, and connected with this momentous occasion and the part in it played by St. Nicholas, there is a legendary story[1] which exhibits a side to his character, if less saintly, at least, more human. The story goes that St. Nicholas at Nice struck an Arian bishop who spoke against the faith and that, for this too violent zeal, he was deprived of the right of wearing bishop's robes. But, the story adds, in celebrating the mass, he saw angels bearing him the miter and the pallium as a sign that Heaven had not blamed his wrath.

The orthodoxy of St. Nicholas is thus put beyond question. If he was a foe to heresy, he was still more a foe to paganism. In the story from the Golden Legend already quoted is recorded his activity in uprooting the worship of Diana in Lycia and the particular hatred of the goddess, or devil as she was conceived of, that he incurred thereby. Concerning his zeal in this work, Wace[2] has the following additional details to offer. "Before the time of St. Nicholas," he tells us, "devils had power. People worshiped gods and goddesses: Phœbus, Jupiter, Mars, Mercury, Diana, Juno, Venus, Minerva. They had painted images with names written on the foreheads. Diana in particular was a she-devil. St. Nicholas broke her image and delivered the people from idolatry."

Naya

St. Nicholas Represented (Byzantine style) in the Mosaics
of St. Mark's in Venice.

But it is particularly in the conflict between Christianity and Mohammedanism that St. Nicholas is prominent as defender of the faith. The time when St. Nicholas worship was introduced in the West was a time when this conflict was at its height, the time of the Crusades. It will be remembered how Jean Bodel in his play, written about the year 1200, made new use of the story of the image of St. Nicholas set as the guardian of treasure. It will be remembered that the setting for the story provided by Bodel was in the wars of Christian against Saracen, and that the central feature of the story in the play is the way in which the Christian image of St. Nicholas proved his power to be greater than that of the Mohammedan idol of Tervagant, and thus led the Mohammedan king with his seneschal and all his emirs to adopt the Christian faith.

In Eastern countries the conflict between Christianity and Mohammedanism, so much alive in Western Europe in the time of the Crusades, continues in active form in our own time. It must be remembered, too, that in Eastern countries St. Nicholas occupies a place even higher than that occupied by him in the West in our time. It is not unnatural, then, that there he should be looked to as the defender of the Christian faith.

How well he is thought to be able to represent the Christian cause is well brought out in a naïvely humorous Albanian folk-tale.[3] The story goes as follows: Mohammed was the guest of St. Nicholas. When the time to eat came around, Mohammed asked where were the servants. St. Nicholas replied that no servants were needed, that at a word from his mouth or a stroke on the table, the edibles would be ready. He then proceeded to demonstrate that what he said was entirely true, causing to appear on the table everything that one could desire to eat and drink.

Mohammed, not to be outdone, on his return home caused his servant to construct a table which would turn and could thus be closed into the wall leaving no visible sign. He commanded his servant to make ready food of every kind, and when he heard a rap, to push the laden table through the wall. He then invited St. Nicholas to his house, intending to exhibit powers as great as those shown by St. Nicholas.

But St. Nicholas made all his plans go awry. He made the servant deaf, so that there was no response to the rap of Mohammed, and St. Nicholas himself had to get up and bring in through the wall the table laden with food, naturally to the discomfiture of his host.

The next day Mohammed invited St. Nicholas again, promising to work a miracle before him. He caused a great number of jugs and cans and dishes of various kinds to be taken to the top of a hill. At a sign from Mohammed, these were to be rolled down the hill and a cannon fired. When St. Nicholas arrived, he bade Mohammed work his miracle. Mohammed raised his hand, and the expected noise followed. St. Nicholas, however, gave no sign of fear. Mohammed then bade him work a miracle. St. Nicholas clapped his hands, and immediately the thunder rolled and the lightning flashed, overwhelming Moham- med with terror.

10

CHAPTER XI

CONCLUSION

A ND when it pleased our Lord to have him depart out of this world, he prayed our Lord that he would send him his angels, and inclining his head, he saw the angels come to him, whereby he knew well that he should depart, and began this holy psalm: *In te domine speravi*, unto *in manus tuas*, and so saying: "Lord into thine hands I commend my spirit," he rendered up his soul and died, the year of our Lord three hundred and forty-three, with great melody sung of the celestial company.

This is the Golden Legend account of the end of the earthly life of the kindly bishop-saint. His body was placed in a tomb of marble, and in the year 1087 was discovered by Italian merchants and borne by them to the city of Bari in Italy. There his tomb is a famous center for pilgrimages. On his festival day, many thousands bearing staves bound with olive and pine honor his memory.[1] It is said that when his tomb at Myra was opened, the body was found swimming in oil, and that to this day there continues to issue from his body a holy oil "which is much available to the health and sicknesses of many men."

St. Nicholas, the guardian of so many things, also keeps guard over his own remains. Wace relates the story of a man carrying off a supposed tooth of the holy saint. In the night St. Nicholas appeared and admonished the thief, and in the morning the tooth was gone.

St. Nicholas was mortal. But his deeds are immortal. His beneficent acts have flowered in legendary story and have found fruition in universal popular customs animated by the same spirit of kindness that pervaded the whole life of the saint. Probably the life history of no other person, save that of the Founder of Christianity himself, has been so intimately woven about human custom and human life as that of St. Nicholas. In certain parts of Siberia he is worshiped as a god. Even in our own country, although we are supposed to have outgrown idolatry, representations of Santa Claus about Christmas time, in shop windows and on street corners, are objects of worship little short of idolatry. To Santa Claus also at Christmas time are addressed the most sincere, even if not the most unselfish, supplications.

We may well conclude our present considera-
tion of St. Nicholas and his works with an invoca-
tion to him, using the words composed by the
recluse Godric, back in the twelfth century, which
form one of the very earliest of English lyrics:

> Sainte Nicholaes, godes druth,
> Tymbre us faire scone hus—
> At thi burth, at thi bare—
> Sainte Nicholaes, bring us wel thare.

NOTES

CHAPTER I

[1] Manchester *Guardian*.

[2] A. Tille, *Die Geschichte der Deutschen Weihnacht*, Leipzig, 1893, p. 30.

[3] O. von Reinsberg-Düringsfeld, *Traditions et Légendes de la Belgique*, p. 302.

[4] Do., p. 323.

[5] Reinsberg-Düringsfeld, *Das festliche Jahr der germanischen Völker*, Leipzig, 1863, pp. 360 ff.

[6] Do., pp. 362, 363.

[7] P. M. Hough, *Dutch Life in Town and Country*, London and New York, 1901, pp. 116 ff.   The present account of St. Nicholas customs in Holland is based on notes from the book by Hough, but is not quoted exactly in order of details nor in wording.

[8] Do., p. 121.

[9] I. von Zingerle, *Zeitschrift für Volkskunde*, ii., 329 ff.

[10] Hough, *op. cit.*, p. 117.

[11] Do., p. 125.

[12] Do., p. 125.

[13] I. von Zingerle, *op. cit.*, p. 343.

[14] Hough, *op. cit.*, p. 125.

[15] Do., p. 126.

[16] Reinsberg-Düringsfeld, *Das festliche Jahr*, p. 362.

[17] Tille, *op. cit.*, p. 35.

[18] Brand, *Popular Antiquities*, i., p. 420.

[19] Tille, *op. cit.*, p. 299.

[20] Do., p. 36.

[21] Do., p. 33.

[22] Do., p. 36.

[23] Do., p. 202.

[24] Reinsberg-Düringsfeld, *Das festliche Jahr*, p. 382; C. A. Miles, *Christmas*, London, 1912, p. 231.

[25] *St. Nicholas, Our Holidays*, New York, 1916, p. 64.

[26] W. A. Wheeler, *Dictionary of Noted Names in Fiction*, Boston, 1883.

[27] Tille, *op. cit.*, p. 119.

[28] Reinsberg-Düringsfeld, *op. cit.*, p. 342.

[29] Reinsberg-Düringsfeld, quoted by Miles, *op. cit.*, p. 277, footnote.

[30] Hough, *op. cit.*, p. 120.

CHAPTER II

[1] G. de Saint Laurent, *Guide de l'Art Chrétien*, 1874, v., p. 349.

[2] A. Butler, *Lives of the Fathers, Martyrs, and other Principal Saints*, London, 1838.

[3] New York *Times*, Oct. 24, 1915.

[4] Mrs. Jameson, *Sacred and Legendary Art*, vol. ii.

CHAPTER III

[1] *The Golden Legend*, Caxton translation, Temple Classics series, vol. ii., pp. 109–122.

[2] Do., pp. 119, 120.

[3] Mrs. Jameson, *op. cit.;* also H. Thode, *Franz von Assisi*, Berlin, 1904.

[4] C. Cahier, *Caractéristiques des saints dans l'art populaire*, Paris, 1867, vol. i.

[5] E. Anichkof, "St. Nicholas and Artemis," *Folk-Lore*, v., pp. 108 ff.

[6] Hough, *op. cit.*, p. 122.

[7] Brand, *op. cit.*, i., p. 417.

CHAPTER IV

[1] Tille, *op. cit.*, p. 32.

[2] Do., p. 300.

[3] Brand, *op. cit.*, i., p. 420.

[4] R. T. Hampson, *Medii Aevi Kalendarium*, London, 1841, ii., p. 76.

[5] T. Wright, *Songs and Carols*, Warton Club, 1856, p. 4.

[6] Brand, *op. cit.*, i., p. 421.

[7] Brady, *Clavis Calendaria*, quoted by W. Hone, *The Every-Day Book*, London, 1838.

[8] New York *Times*, April 18, 1915.

[9] Mrs. Jameson, *op. cit.*

[10] Brand, *op. cit.*, ii., p. 356.

[11] *Encyclopedia Britannica*, article "Pawnbrokers."

[12] *Cf.* the story of the Jew who left his property under the protection of the image of St. Nicholas.

CHAPTER V

[1] Galleria antica e moderna.

[2] C. A. Miles, *op. cit.*, p. 168.

[3] A. F. Leach, "The Schoolboy's Feast," *Fortnightly Review*, vol. lix., pp. 128–141.

[4] E. K. Chambers, *The Mediæval Stage*, London, 1903, i., p. 294. The total amount of the debt to Chambers's work it has not been possible to indicate in these notes.

[5] Do., p. 357.

[6] Do., p. 348.

[7] Brand, *op. cit.*, i., p. 423.

[8] Chambers, *op. cit.*, p. 338.

[9] Tille, *op. cit.*, p. 31, quoted by Chambers.

[10] Reinsberg-Düringsfeld, *Traditions et Légendes de la Belgique*, p. 348.

[11] Leach, *op. cit.*

CHAPTER VI

[1] H. Thode, *Franz von Assisi*, Berlin, 1909.

[2] Verses 1080–1143.

[3] Verses 208–216.

[4] M. Hamilton, *op. cit.*, pp. 47, 48.

CHAPTER VII

[1] G. R. Coffman, *A New Theory concerning the Origin of the Miracle Play*, Univ. of Chicago *diss.*, 1914.

[2] Henry Morley, *English Writers*, 1889, vol. iii., pp. 105–114.

[3] E. Du Meril, *Les Origines Latines du Théâtre Moderne*, new edition, Paris, 1897, pp. 272–276.

[4] C. M. Gayley, *Plays of our Forefathers*, New York, 1907, p. 64.

[5] Du Meril, *op. cit.*, pp. 276–284.

[6] Gaston Paris, *La littérature française au Moyen-Age*, Paris, 1890, §167.

[7] W. Creizenach, *Geschichte des neueren dramas*, Halle, 1893, i., pp. 139–141.

CHAPTER VIII

[1] E. Bisland and A. Hoyt, *Seekers in Sicily.*

[2] Brand, *op. cit.*, pp. 363, 364.

[3] Do., pp. 363, 364.

[4] H. F. Feilberg, *Jul,* Copenhagen, 1909, i., p. 105.

[5] C. Cahier, *op. cit.*

[6] This additional list is derived from somewhat scattered references in works cited above by Brand and by Cahier.

[7] M. Hamilton, *op. cit.*, pp. 29, 30.

[8] E. Anichkof, *op. cit.*, pp. 108 ff.

[9] Brand, *op. cit.*, i., p. 419.

[10] Anichkof, *op. cit.*

[11] Zingerle, *op. cit.*, p. 334.

[12] Anichkof, *op. cit.*, p. 109.

[13] First part of *Henry IV.*, Act II., scene i.

[14] Brand, *op. cit.*, i., p. 418.   *Cf.* also the Oxford Dictionary under Nicholas.

[15] T. Wright, *op. cit.*, p. 99.

CHAPTER IX

[1] M. Hamilton, *op. cit.*, p. 16.

[2] Do., p. 13.

[3] Do., p. 18.

[4] Do., p. 20.

[5] Do., p. 33.

[6] Do., p. 34.

[7] Do., p. 31.

[8] J. C. Lawson, *Modern Greek Folk-Lore and Ancient Greek Religion*, Cambridge, 1910, p. 135.

[9] M. Hamilton, *op. cit.*, p. 30.

[10] E. Anichkof, *op. cit.*, p. 114.

[11] Do., pp. 115, 116.

[12] Hampson, *op. cit.*, p. 68.

[13] Keightley, *Fairy Mythology*, i., pp. 234, 235, quoted by Hampson, *op. cit.*, p. 75.

[14] *Revue des traditions populaires*, i., p. 7, quoted by Anichkof.

[15] This is the main thesis of the article by Anichkof.

[16] J. W. Wolf, Hocker, and Al Kaufmann, quoted by Zingerle, *op. cit.*, p. 331.

[17] A. Tille, *Yule and Christmas*, London, 1899, p. 115; H. Feilberg, *Jul*, Copenhagen, 1904, ii., p. 179.

[18] C. A. Miles, *op. cit.*, p. 221.

CHAPTER X

[1] C. Cahier, *op. cit.*

[2] Wace, *op. cit.*, vv. 342 ff.

[3] J. V. Jarnik, *Zeitschrift für Volkskunde*, ii., pp. 348, 349.

CHAPTER XI

[1] Miles, *op. cit.*, p. 221.